CBSE Term II 2022

Computer Science

Class XI

 Complete Theory Covering NCERT

Case Based Questions

Short/Long Answer Type Questions

3 Practice Papers with Explanations

Author
Neetu Gaikwad

arihant

ARIHANT PRAKASHAN (School Division Series)

arihant

ARIHANT PRAKASHAN (School Division Series)

ꜱ **Administrative & Production Offices**

Regd. Office

'Ramchhaya' 4577/15, Agarwal Road, Darya Ganj, New Delhi -110002
Tele: 011- 47630600, 43518550

ꜱ **Head Office**

Kalindi, TP Nagar, Meerut (UP) - 250002, Tel: 0121-7156203, 7156204

ꜱ **Sales & Support Offices**

Agra, Ahmedabad, Bengaluru, Bareilly, Chennai, Delhi, Guwahati, Hyderabad, Jaipur, Jhansi, Kolkata, Lucknow, Nagpur & Pune.

ꜱ **ISBN :** 978-93-25796-87-4

ꜱ **PRICE :** ₹125.00

PO No : TXT-XX-XXXXXXX-X-XX

Published by Arihant Publications (India) Ltd.

For further information about the books published by Arihant, log on to www.arihantbooks.com or e-mail at info@arihantbooks.com

Follow us on   

Contents

Syllabus

CBSE Term II Class XI

Computer Science

		Marks
2.	Computational Thinking and Programming - 1	20
3.	Society, Law and Ethics	15
	Total	**35**

UNIT II: COMPUTATIONAL THINKING AND PROGRAMMING – 1

- Lists: introduction, indexing, list operations (concatenation, repetition, membership & slicing), traversing a list using loops, built-in functions: len(), list(), append(), extend(), insert(), count(), index(), remove(), pop(), reverse(), sort(), sorted(), min(), max(), sum(); nested lists, suggested programs: finding the maximum, minimum, mean of numeric values stored in a list; linear search on list of numbers and counting the frequency of elements in a list

- Tuples: introduction, indexing, tuple operations (concatenation, repetition, membership & slicing), built-in functions: len(), tuple(), count(), index(), sorted(), min(), max(), sum(); tuple assignment, nested tuple, suggested programs: finding the minimum, maximum, mean of values stored in a tuple; linear search on a tuple of numbers, counting the frequency of elements in a tuple

- Dictionary: introduction, accessing items in a dictionary using keys, mutability of dictionary (adding a new item, modifying an existing item), traversing a dictionary, built-in functions: len(), dict(), keys(), values(), items(), get(), update(), del(), clear(), fromkeys(), copy(), pop(), popitem(), setdefault(), max(), min(), count(), sorted(), copy(); suggested programs : count the number of times a character appears in a given string using a dictionary, create a dictionary with names of employees, their salary and access them

- Introduction to Python modules: Importing module using 'import <module>' and using from statement, Importing math module (pi, e, sqrt, ceil, floor, pow, fabs, sin, cos, tan); random module (random, randint, randrange), statistics module (mean, median, mode)

• UNIT III: SOCIETY, LAW AND ETHICS

- Digital Footprints

- Digital society and Netizen: net etiquettes, communication etiquettes, social media etiquettes

- Data protection: Intellectual Property Right (copyright, patent, trademark), violation of IPR (plagiarism, copyright infringement, trademark infringement), open source softwares and licensing (Creative Commons, GPL and Apache)

- Cyber-crime: definition, hacking, eavesdropping, phishing and fraud emails, ransomware, preventing cyber crime

- Cyber safety: safely browsing the web, identity protection, confidentiality, cyber trolls and bullying.

- Safely accessing web sites: malware, viruses, Trojans, adware

- E-waste management: proper disposal of used electronic gadgets

- Indian Information Technology Act (IT Act)

- Technology & Society: Gender and disability issues while teaching and using computers

CBSE Circular

Acad - 51/2021, 05 July 2021

Exam Scheme Term I & II

Special Scheme for 2021-22

A. Academic session to be divided into 2 Terms with approximately 50% syllabus in each term:

The syllabus for the Academic session 2021-22 will be divided into 2 terms by following a systematic approach by looking into the interconnectivity of concepts and topics by the Subject Experts and the Board will conduct examinations at the end of each term on the basis of the bifurcated syllabus. This is done to increase the probability of having a Board conducted classes X and XII examinations at the end of the academic session.

B. The syllabus for the Board examination 2021-22 will be rationalized similar to that of the last academic session to be notified in July 2021. For academic transactions, however, schools will follow the curriculum and syllabus released by the Board vide Circular no. F.1001/CBSE-Acad/Curriculum/2021 dated 31 March 2021. Schools will also use alternative academic calendar and inputs from the NCERT on transacting the curriculum.

C. Efforts will be made to make Internal Assessment/ Practical/ Project work more credible and valid as per the guidelines and Moderation Policy to be announced by the Board to ensure fair distribution of marks.

Details of Curriculum Transaction

- Schools will continue teaching in distance mode till the authorities permit in-person mode of teaching in schools.

- **Classes IX-X: Internal Assessment** (throughout the year-irrespective of Term I and II) would include the *3 periodic tests, student enrichment, portfolio and practical work/ speaking listening activities/ project.*

- **Classes XI-XII: Internal Assessment** (throughout the year-irrespective of Term I and II) would include end of topic or unit tests/ exploratory activities/ practicals/ projects.

- Schools would create a student profile for all assessment undertaken over the year and retain the evidences in digital format.

- CBSE will facilitate schools to upload marks of Internal Assessment on the CBSE IT platform.

- Guidelines for Internal Assessment for all subjects will also be released along with the rationalized term wise divided syllabus for the session 2021-22.The Board would also provide additional resources like sample assessments, question banks, teacher training etc. for more reliable and valid internal assessments.

केन्द्रीय माध्यमिक शिक्षा बोर्ड

(शिक्षा मंत्रालय, भारत सरकार के अधीन एक स्वायत संगठन)

CENTRAL BOARD OF SECONDARY EDUCATION

(An Autonomous Organisation under the Ministryof Education, Govt. of India)

Term I Examinations:

- At the end of the first term, the Board will organize **Term I Examination** in a flexible schedule to be conducted between November-December 2021 with a window period of 4-8 weeks for schools situated in different parts of country and abroad. Dates for conduct of examinations will be notified subsequently.

- The Question Paper will have Multiple Choice Questions (MCQ) including case-based MCQs and MCQs on assertion-reasoning type. Duration of test will be **90 minutes** and it will cover only the rationalized syllabus of **Term I only** (i.e. approx. 50% of the entire syllabus).

- Question Papers will be sent by the CBSE to schools along with marking scheme.

- The exams will be conducted under the supervision of the External Center Superintendents and Observers appointed by CBSE.

- The responses of students will be captured on OMR sheets which, after scanning may be directly uploaded at CBSE portal or alternatively may be evaluated and marks obtained will be uploaded by the school on the very same day. The final direction in this regard will be conveyed to schools by the Examination Unit of the Board.

- Marks of the **Term I** Examination will contribute to the final overall score of students.

Term II Examination/ Year-end Examination:

- At the end of the second term, the Board would organize **Term II or Year-end Examination** based on the rationalized syllabus of Term II only (i.e. approximately 50% of the entire syllabus).

- This examination would be held around **March-April 2022** at the examination centres fixed by the Board.

- The paper will be of **2 hours duration** and have questions of different formats (case-based/ situation based, open ended- short answer/ long answer type).

- In case the situation is not conducive for normal descriptive examination **a 90 minute MCQ based exam** will be conducted at the end of the Term II also.

- Marks of the Term II Examination would contribute to the final overall score.

To cover this situation, we have given both MCQs and Subjective Questions in each Chapter.

6. <u>Assessment / Examination as per different situations</u>

A. In case the situation of the pandemic improves and students are able to come to schools or centres for taking the exams.

Board would conduct Term I and Term II examinations at schools/centres and the theory marks will be distributed equally between the two exams.

B. In case the situation of the pandemic forces complete closure of schools during November-December 2021, but Term II exams are held at schools or centres.

Term I MCQ based examination would be done by students online/offline from home - in this case, the weightage of this exam for the final score would be reduced, and weightage of Term II exams will be increased for declaration of final result.

C. In case the situation of the pandemic forces complete closure of schools during March-April 2022, but Term I exams are held at schools or centres.

Results would be based on the performance of students on Term I MCQ based examination and internal assessments. The weightage of marks of Term I examination conducted by the Board will be increased to provide year end results of candidates.

D. In case the situation of the pandemic forces complete closure of schools and Board conducted Term I and II exams are taken by the candidates from home in the session 2021-22.

Results would be computed on the basis of the Internal Assessment/Practical/Project Work and Theory marks of Term-I and II exams taken by the candidate from home in Class X / XII subject to the moderation or other measures to ensure validity and reliability of the assessment.

In all the above cases, data analysis of marks of students will be undertaken to ensure the integrity of internal assessments and home based exams.

Dr. Joseph Emmanuel
Director (Academics)

CHAPTER 01

Lists in Python

In this Chapter...

- Creating a List
- Accessing Lists
- Traversing a List
- Comparison Operators

- Membership Operators
- List Operations
- Built-in Functions

In Python, list is a type of container in data structures, which is used to store multiple data at the same time. List acts as an array which defined other languages such as C++, Java etc. List contains a sequence of heterogeneous elements which makes it powerful tool in Python. It can store integer, string as well as object in a single list. It is also useful for implementing stacks and queues.

Lists are mutable which means they can be changed after creation. Each element of a list is assigned a number its position or index. The first index is 0, the second index is 1, the third index is 2 and so on.

Each element in the list has its definite place, which allows duplicating of elements in the list with each element having its own distinct place and credibility.

Creating a List

In Python, lists can be created to put the elements in square brackets [ ]. The elements in the list are separated by the comma (,).

For example,

$$a = [34, 76, 11, 98]$$
$$b = ['s', 3, 6, 't']$$
$$c = [34, 0.5, 75]$$
$$d = [ ]$$

Creating a List From an Existing Sequence

In Python, list ( ) method is used to create list from an existing sequence.

Syntax

```
new_list_name = list (sequence/string)
```

Here, sequence includes tuples, lists etc.

For example,

```
>>>A = "PYTHON"
>>>A1 = list(A)
>>>A1
['P', 'Y', 'T', 'H', 'O', 'N']
>>>A = list("PYTHON")
>>>A
['P', 'Y', 'T', 'H', 'O', 'N']
>>>1 = ('P', 'Y', 'T', 'H', 'O', 'N')
>>>11 = list(1)
>>>11
['P', 'Y', 'T', 'H', 'O', 'N']
```

Or

list ( ) method is also used to create list of characters and integers through keyboard.

For example,

```
>>> a= list(input ("Enter the elements :"))
Enter the elements : 234576
>>>a
['2', '3', '4', '5', '7', '6']
>>>b = list(input("Enter string : "))
Enter the string : ARIHANT
>>>b
['A', 'R', 'I', 'H', 'A', 'N', 'T']
```

We can create different types of list in Python as follows:

(i) Empty List

Empty list can be created in Python using [ ]. Here is the two ways to create empty list as

(a) ```>>>a = [ ]```
```>>>print (a)```
Output
```[ ]```

(b) ```>>>a = list ( )```
```>>>print (a)```
Output
```[ ]```

(ii) Mixed Data Types List

It can be created to place different data types such as integers, strings, double etc., into one list.

For example,
```>>>a = ['Neha', 'Sharma', 25, 75, 6, 47]```
```>>>print(a)```

Output

['Neha', 'Sharma', 25, 75, 6, 47]

(iii) Nested List

Nested lists are list objects where the elements in the lists can be lists themselves.

For example,
```>>> A = ['Neha', 4, 1, [5, 23, 4], 98]```
```>> print (A)```

Output

['Neha', 4, 1, [5, 23, 4], 98]

List A contains 5 elements while inner list contains 3 elements ([5, 23, 4]). List A is considered [5, 23, 4] as one element.

Accessing Lists

To access the list's elements, index number is used. Use the index operator [ ] to access the elements of a list. The index should be an integer. Index of 0 refers to first element, 1 refers to second element and so on. While the index of -1 refers to the first last element, -2 refers to the second last element and so on.

For example,
```11 = [5, 7, 3, 4, 5, 6, 9, 0, 8]```

It is called positive index

0	1	2	3	4	5	6	7	8
5	7	3	4	5	6	9	0	8
-9	-8	-7	-6	-5	-4	-3	-2	-1

It is called negative index

```>>>11 = [34, 87, 'Computer', 12, 'Python',```
```11, 76, 'Option']```

```>>>11 [0]```
```34```
```>>>11 [6]```
```76```
```>>>11 [-4]```
```'Python'```
```>>>11 [3]```
```12```
```>>>11 [-3]```
```11```
```>>>11 [9]```

It will give an error as ```IndexError: list index out of range```. Because it has 9 elements for which indexing are 0 to 8.

Difference between String and List

Strings are immutable which means the values provided to them will not change in the program.

a = "Here is string"

You can extract value using index, find values but cannot modify it.

While lists are mutable which means the values of list can be changed at any point of time.

a = [1, 2, 3]

You have some methods associated with lists like– append, pop, extend etc.

$a[1:1] = [5, 6]$, then 'a' will be [1, 5, 6, 2, 3].

Traversing a List

Traversing a list is a technique to access an individual element of that list. It is also called **iterate over a list**.

There are multiple ways to iterate over a list in Python. These are as follows

Using for loop

The most common and easy way to traverse a list is with for loop. for loop is used when you want to traverse each element of a list.

Syntax ```for variable in list_name:```

For example,
```a = ['P', 'R', 'O', 'G', 'R', 'A', 'M']```
```for i in a:```
```   print (i)```

Output
P
R
O
G
R
A
M
```

Using for loop with range ( )

There is another method to traverse a list using for loop with range( ). This is also used len( ) function with range. This method is used when you want to traverse particular characters in a list.

Syntax `for variable in range (len(list_name)):`

For example,
```
a = ['P', 'R', 'O', 'G', 'R', 'A', 'M']
for i in range (len (a)):
    print (a [i])
```

Output

P
R
O
G
R
A
M

Program to display the elements of list
['P', 'Y', 'T', 'H', 'O', 'N']
in separate line with their index number.

For example,
```
list1 = ['P', 'Y', 'T', 'H', 'O', 'N']
L1 = len (list1)
for i in range (L1) :
    print("Element :", list1 [i], "at index
                                number", i)
```

Output

Element : P at index number 0
Element : Y at index number 1
Element : T at index number 2
Element : H at index number 3
Element : O at index number 4
Element : N at index number 5

Comparison Operators

A comparison operator in Python, also called Python relational operator ($<, >, = =, ! = , > = , < =$) that compare the values of two operands and returns True or False based on whether the condition is met.

Comparison operators for comparing lists are as follows

Less than (<) operator

It checks if the left value is lesser than that on the right.

For example,
```
>>>a = [1, 2, 3, 4]
>>>b = [5, 2, 3, 4]
>>>a < b
    True
```

It gives True, which get from first element from two lists as 1 < 5.

Greater than (>) operator

It checks whether the left value is greater than that on the right.

For example,
```
>>>a = [1, 2, 3, 4]
>>>b = [5, 2, 3, 4]
>>>a > b
    False
```

It gives False, which get from first element from two lists as 1 > 5.

Less than or Equal to (<=) operator

This operator returns True only, if the value on the left is either less than or equal to that on the right of the operator.

For example,
```
>>>a = [2, 4, 3, 7]
>>>b = [3, 4, 5, 7]
>>>a <= b
    True
```

Greater than or Equal to (>=) operator

This operator returns True only, if the value on the left is greater than or equal to that on the right of the operator.

For example,
```
>>>a = [4, 3, 6, 8]
>>>b = [2, 5, 4, 3]
>>>a >= b
    True
```

Equal to (= =) operator

This operator returns True, if the values on either side of the operator are equal.

For example,
```
>>>a = [2, 3, 4, 6]
>>>b = [2, [3, 4], 6]
>>>c = [2, 3, 4, 6]
>>>a == b
    False
>>>a == c
    True
```

Not equal (! =) operator

This operator returns True, if the values on either side of the operator are unequal.

For example,
```
>>>a = [2, 3, 4, 6]
>>>b = [2, [3, 4], 6]
>>>a != b
    True
```

Membership Operators

These operators are used to find out whether a value is a member of a sequence such as string, list, tuple, dictionary etc.

There are two types of membership operator as follows

in operator

It evaluates True, if the value in the left operand appears in the sequence found in the right operand.

For example,
```
l1 = [45, 76, [3, 98], 6]
l2 = [60, [23, 43], 65]
for item in l1:
    if item in l2:
        print ("Exist")
else :
    print ("Not Exist")
```

Output

Not Exist

not in operator

It evaluates True, if the value in the left operand does not appear in the sequence found in the right operand.

For example,
```
a = 54
b = 87
list1 = [45, 65, 30, 78, 512, 87]
if (a not in list1):
    print ("a is NOT present in given list")
else :
    print ("a is present in given list")
if (b in list1):
    print ("b is present in given list")
else :
    print ("b is NOT present in given list")
```

Output

a is NOT present in given list

b is present in given list

List Operations

We can perform various operations on list in Python, some of them are describe below

Concatenate Lists

The most conventional method to perform on the list concatenaton, the use of (+) operator can easily add the whole of one list to other list and hence perform the concatenation.

Syntax `list = list1 + list2`

For example,
```
>>>l1 = [43, 56, 34]
>>>l2 = [22, 34, 98]
>>>l = l1 + l2
```
```
>>>l
[43, 56, 34, 22, 34, 98]
```
The (+) operator cannot add list with other type as number or string because this operator is used only with list types.

For example,
```
>>>l1 = [2, 5, 7]
>>>l = l1 + 5
Trackback (most recent call last) :
File "<pyshell#5>", line 1, in <module>
    l = l1 + 5
TypeError : can only concatenate list (not
                            "int") to list.
```

For example,
```
>>>l1 = [3, 2, 6]
>>>l = l1 + "Try"
Trackback (most recent call last):
File "<pyshell#1>", line 1, in <module>
    l = l1 + "Try"
TypeError : can only concatenate list (not
                            "str") to list.
```

Replicating List

You can repeat the elements of the list using (*) operator. This operator is used to replicate the list.

Syntax `list = list1 * digit`

For example,
```
>>>l1 = [3, 2, 6]
>>>l = l1 * 2
>>>l
[3, 2, 6, 3, 2, 6]
```

Slicing of a List

In Python list, there are multiple ways to print the whole list with all the elements, but to print a specific range of elements from the list, we use slice operation. Slice operation is performed on lists with the use of colon (:).

Syntax `s = list_name [Start : End]`

For example,
```
>>>list1 = [4, 3, 7, 6, 4, 9, 5, 0, 3, 2]
>>>s = list1 [2 : 5]
>>>s
[7, 6, 4]
```
To print elements from beginning to a range use [: Index], to print elements from end use [: –Index] and to print elements from specific index till the end use [Index :].

For example,
```
>>>list1 = [4, 3, 7, 6, 4, 9, 5, 0, 3, 2]
>>>s = list1 [: 5]
>>>s
[4, 3, 7, 6, 4]
>>>s = list1 [: –6]
>>>s
[4, 3, 7, 6]
>>>s = list1 [3 :]
```

```
>>>s
[6, 4, 9, 5, 0, 3, 2]
```
You can also print all elements of list in reverse order using [: : −1].

For example,
```
>>>s = list1 [: : -1]
>>>s
[2, 3, 0, 5, 9, 4, 6, 7, 3, 4]
```
Lists are also provide slice steps which used to extract elements from list that are not consecutive.

Syntax `s = list_name [Start : Stop : Step]`

It takes three parameters which are as follows

- **Start** starting integer where the slicing of the object starts.
- **Stop** integer until which the slicing takes place. The slicing stops at index −1.
- **Step** integer value which determines the increment between each index for slicing.

For example,
```
>>>list1 = [4, 3, 7, 6, 4, 9, 5, 0, 3, 2]
>>>l1 = list1 [1 : 10 : 3]
>>>l1
[3, 4, 0]
>>>l2 = list1 [2 : 12 : 2]
>>>l2
[7, 4, 5, 3]
>>>l3 = list1 [::4]
>>>l3
[4, 4, 3]
>>>l4 = list1 [::8]
>>>l4
[4, 3]
>>>l5 = list1 [3 ::]
>>>l5
[6, 4, 9, 5, 0, 3, 2]
```

For example,

Python program to count the number of elements in a given range using traversal and multiple line code.
```
c = 0
l = 40
r = 80
list1 = [10, 20, 30, 40, 50, 40, 40, 60, 70]
for x  in list1 :
    if x >= l and x <= r:
        c + = 1
        print("List:", list1)
        print("Elements in a list1:", c)
```
Output

List : [10, 20, 30, 40, 50, 40, 40, 60, 70]

Elements in a list1 : 6

List Modification using Slicing

List can be modified after it created using slicing.

For example,
```
>>>l1 = [2, 4, "Try", 54, "Again"]
>>>l1 [0 : 1] = [34, "Hello"]
>>>l1
[34, 'Hello', 4, 'Try', 54, 'Again']
>>>l1 [4] = ["World"]
>>>l1
[34, 'Hello', 4, 'Try', ['World'], 'Again']
>>>l1 [2] = "Hiiii"
>>>l1
[34, 'Hello', 'Hiiii', 'Try', ['World'],
                                'Again']
```

Built-in Functions

Python has large number of built-in functions and methods that make programming easier.

Some of them are as follows

(i) append ( )

This method is used for appending and adding elements to a list. It is used to add elements to the last position of a list.

Syntax `list_name.append (element)`

For example,
```
>>>l1 = [34, 65, 23, 98]
>>>l1.append (76)
>>>l1
[34, 65, 23, 98, 76]
```

(ii) insert ( )

This method is used to insert an element at specified position in the list. This method takes two arguments : one for index number and second for element value.

Syntax `list_name. insert (index, element)`

For example,
```
>>>l1 = [34, 65, 23, 98]
>>>l1.insert (3, 'New')
>>>l1
[34, 65, 23, 'New', 98]
```

(iii) extend ( )

This method is used to add contents of list 2 to the end of list 1.

Syntax `listname1. extend (list_name2)`

For example,
```
>>>l1 = [43, 'Hello', 56]
>>>l2 = ['World', 'Try', 65,77]
>>>l1.extend(l2)
>>>l1
[43, 'Hello', 56, 'World', 'Try', 65, 77]
```

(iv) sum ( )

This method is used to calculate the sum of all the elements in the list.

Syntax `sum (list_name)`

For example,

```
>>>l = [45, 23, 87, 5, 9]
>>>sum (l)
169
```

sum ( ) method is used for only numeric values otherwise it gives an error.

```
>>>l = [45, 23, 87, 5, 'Hello']
>>>sum (l)
Trackback (most recent call last) :
File "<pyshell# 17>", line 1, in <module>
    sum(l)
TypeError: unsupported operand type (s) for
                          + : 'int' and 'str'
```

(v) count ( )

This method is used to calculate total occurrence of given element of list.

Syntax `list_name. count (element)`

For example,

```
>>>list1 = [4, 3, 5, 2, 54, 4, 2, 6, 4, 4, 5]
>>>list1. count(4)
4
```

(vi) len ( )

This method is used to calculate the total length of list.

Syntax `len (list_name)`

For example,

```
>>>list1 = [4, 3, 5, 2, 54, 4, 2, 6, 4, 4, 5]
>>>len (list1)
11
```

(vii) index ()

It returns the index of first occurrence. Start and end index are not necessary parameters.

Syntax `list_name.index (element[, start [, end]])`

For example,

```
>>>list1 = [3, 'New', 2, 6, 'Hello', 2]
>>>list1.index ('Hello')
4
```

(viii) min ( )

It is used to return the minimum element out of elements of list.

Syntax `min (list_name)`

For example,

```
>>>l1 = [45, 87, 23, 90, 12]
>>>min (l1)
12
>>>l2 = ['A', 'B', 'c', 'e', 'a']
>>>min (l2)
'A'
```

It will return min value of character using ASCII value.

```
>>>l3 = ['Rahul', 'Shiv', 'Sandhaya', 'Ankit']
>>>min (l3)
'Ankit'
```

(ix) max ( )

It is used to return the maximum element out of elements of list.

Syntax `max (list_name)`

For example,

```
>>>l1 = [34, 76, 89, 33, 54, 65]
>>>max (l1)
89
>>>l2 = ['t', 'e', 'E', 'U', 'v']
>>>max (l2)
'v'
```

It will return max value of character using ASCII value.

(x) reverse ( )

Using the reverse ( ) method, we can reverse the contents of the list object in-place, i.e. we don't need to create a new list instead we just copy the existing elements to the original list in reverse order.

Syntax `list_name. reverse ( )`

For example,

```
>>>list1 = [34, 76, 89, 33, 54, 65]
>>>list1. reverse( )
>>>print (list1)
[65, 54, 33, 89, 76, 34]
>>>l = ['Hii', 'Hello', 'Hey', 'Namesty']
>>>l.reverse ( )
>>>print (l)
['Namesty', 'Hey', 'Hello', 'Hii']
```

(xi) pop ( )

This function is used to remove the element and return last value from the list or the given index value.

Syntax `list_name.pop (index)`

For example,

```
>>>l1 = [34, 65, 22, 90, 87, 61]
>>>l1.pop (3)
90
>>>print (l1)
[34, 65, 22, 87, 61]
```

If you do not give any index value, then it will remove last value from the list.

```
>>>l1. pop ( )
61
>>>print (l1)
[34, 65, 22, 87]
```

(xii) remove ( )

This method searches for the given element in the list and removes the first matching element. It takes a single element as an argument and remove it from the list.

Syntax `list_name. remove (element)`

For example,
```
>>>list1 = [34, 76, 11, 98, 26, 20]
>>>list1.remove (11)
>>>list1
[34, 76, 98, 26, 20]
>>>l1 = ['Maths', 'English', 'Hindi',
'History', 'Science']
>>>l1.remove('History')
>>>l1
['Maths', 'English', 'Hindi', 'Science']
```

If the element (argument) passed to the remove ( ) method does not exist, ValueError exception is thrown.
```
>>>l1. remove ( )
Trackback (most recent call last) :
File "<pyshell# 11>", line 1, in <module>
    l1.remove ( )
TypeError : remove ( ) takes exactly one
argument (0 given)
```

(xiii) clear ( )

This function is used to remove all the items of a list. This method will empty the entire list.

Syntax `list_name. clear ( )`

For example,
```
>>>l1 = [23, 45, 87, 12, 98]
>>>l1.clear( )
>>>l1
[ ]
```

(xiv) sort ()

This function is used to sort the given list in ascending order.

Syntax `list _name. sort ( )`

For example,
```
>>>list1 = [23, 65, 77, 23, 90, 99, 12]
>>>list1. sort ( )
>>>print (list1)
[12, 23, 23, 65, 77, 90, 99]
>>>list2 = ['abc' 'gdr', 'uyt', 'abc','nki']
>>>list2. sort ( )
>>>print (list2)
['abc', 'abc', 'gdr', 'nki', 'uyt']
```

The sort function has an argument called reverse = True. This allows us to sort the list elements in descending order.

Syntax `list _ name. sort (reverse = True)`

For example,
```
>>>list1 = [23, 65, 77, 23, 90, 99, 12]
>>>list1. sort (reverse = True)
>>>print (list1)
[99, 90, 77, 65, 23, 23, 12]
```

(xv) list ()

It takes sequence types and converts them to lists. This is used to convert a given sequence (tuple/list/string) into list.

Syntax `list (seq)`

For example,
```
>>>t1 = ('Hello', 34, 54, 'xyz')
>>>list1 = list(t1)
>>>print (list1)
['Hello', 34, 54, 'xyz']
>>>t1 = ( )
>>>list1 = list (t1)
>>>print (list1)
[]
```

Chapter Practice

Objective Questions

• Multiple Choice Questions

1. Which value is used to represent the first index of list?

  (a) 1   (b) 0

  (c) −1   (d) a

Ans. (b) To access the list's elements, index number is used. The index number should be an integer. Index of 0 refers to first element, 1 refers to second element and so on.

2. Choose the output of following Python code.

```
l1 = list ()
print (l1)
```

  (a) []   (b) ()

  (c) [,]   (d) Empty

Ans. (a) Empty list can be created in Python using []. To create empty list, list () is also used.

3. Suppose list

```
l1 = [10, 20, 30, 40, 50, 60, 70]
print(l1 [−3])
```

  (a) 30   (b) 50

  (c) 40   (d) Error

Ans. (b) The index of −1 refers to the last element, −2 refers to the second last element and so on. Hence, −3 refers to third last element, i.e. 50.

4. Choose the output from following code.

```
list1 = ['A', 'R', 'I', 'H', 'A', 'N', 'T']
print (list1 [7])
```

  (a) T   (b) N

  (c) A   (d) Error

Ans. (d) In the given code, we are trying to access 8th element from the list which does not exist as we are having total 7 elements for which the last index is 6. So, Python will give an IndexError.

5. Which function is used to insert an element at specified position in the list?

  (a) extend ()   (b) append ()

  (c) insert ()   (d) add ()

Ans. (c) insert () function is used to insert an element at specified position in the list. This method takes two arguments : one for index number and second for element value.

Syntax `list_name.insert(index, element)`

6. Choose the correct option for the following.

```
l1 = [2, 5, 7]
l = l1 + 5
print (l)
```

  (a) [7, 10, 12]

  (b) [2, 5, 7, 5]

  (c) [5, 2, 5, 7]

  (d) TypeError

Ans. (d) + operator cannot add list with other type as number or string because this operator is used only with list types.

So, it will give TypeError as it can only concatenate list (not "int") to list.

7. What is the output of following code?

```
l1 = [3, 2, 6]
l = l1 * 2
print (l)
```

  (a) [3, 2, 6, 3, 2, 6]

  (b) [6, 4, 12]

  (c) [3, 4, 12]

  (d) TypeError

Ans. (a) * operator can repeat the elements of the list.

Syntax `list = list1 * digit`

8. Which of the following is true regarding lists in Python?

  (a) Lists are immutable.

  (b) Size of the lists must be specified before its initialisation.

  (c) Elements of lists are stored in contiguous memory location.

  (d) size(list1) command is used to find the size of lists.

Ans. (c) Elements of lists are stored in contiguous memory location, so it is true regarding lists in Python.

9. Suppose list1 is [56, 89, 75, 65, 99], what is the output of list1 [− 2]?

  (a) Error   (b) 75

  (c) 99   (d) 65

Ans. (d) −1 corresponds to the last index in the list, −2 represents the second last element and so on.

So, the output for list1 [− 2] is 65 because 65 is second last element of list1.

10. Identify the output of following code.
```
List1=[1, 2, 3, 7, 9]
L=List1.pop(9)
print(L)
```
(a) Syntax error   (b) 9

(c) [1, 2, 3, 7]   (d) None of these

Ans. (*a*) In pop(9), parentheses put index number instead of element. In the given list, maximum index number is 4, then 9 is out of index range.

11. Suppose list1 is [2445,133,12454,123], what is the output of max(list1)?

(a) 2445   (b) 133

(c) 12454   (d)123

Ans. (*c*) max() returns the maximum element in the list. From given options, 12454 is the element with maximum value.

12. To add a new element to a list, which command will we use?
```
(a) list1.add(8)
(b) list1.append(8)
(c) list1.addLast(8)
(d) list1.addEnd(8)
```
Ans. (*b*) We use the function append() to add an element to the list.

13. What will be the output of the following Python code?
```
list1=[9, 5, 3, 5, 4]
list1[1:2]=[7,8]
print(list1)
```
(a) [9,5, 3, 7, 8]   (b) [9, 7, 8, 3, 5, 4]

(c) [9,[7, 8], 3, 5,4]   (d) Error

Ans. (*b*) In the piece of code, slice assignment has been implemented. The sliced list is replaced by the assigned elements in the list.

14. Consider the declaration a=[2, 3, 'Hello', 23.0]. Which of the following represents the data type of 'a'?

(a) String   (b) Tuple

(c) Dictionary   (d) List

Ans. (*d*) List contains a sequence of heterogeneous elements which store integer, string as well as object. It can created to put elements separated by comma (,) in square brackets [].

15. Identify the output of the following Python statement.
```
x = [[1, 2, 3, 4], [5, 6, 7, 8]]
y = x [0] [2]
print(y)
```
(a) 3   (b) 4

(c) 6   (d) 7

Ans. (*a*) x is a list, which has two sub-lists in it. Elements of first list will be represented by [0] [i] and elements of second list will be represented by [1] [i].

16. Which method will empty the entire list?

(a) pop()   (b) clear()

(c) sort()   (d) remove()

Ans. (*b*) clear() method is used to remove all the items of a list. This method will empty the entire list.

Syntax
```
list_name.clear()
```

17. Which of the following allows us to sort the list elements in descending order?

(a) reverse = True

(b) reverse = False

(c) sort (descending)

(d) sort. descending

Ans. (*a*) sort() is used to sort the given list in ascending order. The sort() has an argument called reverse = True. This allows us to sort the list elements in descending order.

18. Identify the correct output.
```
>>>11 = [34, 65, 23, 98]
>>>11. insert(2, 55)
>>> 11
```
(a) [34, 65, 23, 55]   (b) [34, 55, 65, 23, 98]

(c) [34, 65, 55, 98]   (d) [34, 65, 55, 23, 98]

Ans. (*d*) insert() is used to insert an element at specified position in the list. This method takes two arguments : one for index number and second for element value.

Syntax
```
list_name.insert(index, element)
```

19. Find the output from the following code.
```
list1=[2, 5, 4, 7, 7, 7, 8, 90]
del list1[2 : 4]
print(list1)
```
(a) [2, 5, 7, 7, 8, 90]   (b) [5, 7, 7, 7, 8, 90]

(c) [2, 5, 4, 8, 90]   (d) Error

Ans. (*a*) del keyword is used to delete the elements from the list.

20. Slice operation is performed on lists with the use of

(a) semicolon   (b) comma

(c) colon   (d) hash

Ans. (*c*) In Python list, there are multiple ways to print the whole list with all the elements, but to print a specific range of elements from the list, we use slice operation. Slice operation is performed on lists with the use of colon (:).

• Case Based MCQs

21. Suppose that list L1
```
["Hello", ["am", "an"], ["that", "the",
"this"], "you", "we", "those", "these"]
```
Based on the above information, answer the following questions.

(i) Find the output of len (L1).

(a) 10   (b) 7

(c) 6   (d) Error

(ii) Find the output of L1[3 : 5].
  (a) ["that", "the", "this"]   (b) ["we", "those"]
  (c) ["you", "we"]   (d) [you, we]

(iii) What will be the output of L1[5:] +L1[2]?
  (a) ['those', 'these', 'that', 'the', 'this']
  (b) ['those', 'these']
  (c) ['that', 'the', 'this']
  (d) Error

(iv) Choose the correct output of
```
print (L1[6:])
```
  (a) "those"   (b) "these"
  (c) "those", "these"   (d) None of these

(v) Give the correct statement for
```
['Hello', ['am', 'an'], ['that', 'the',
'this'], 'you', 'we', 'those', 'these']
```
  (a) L1[]   (b) L1[:]
  (c) all.L1()   (d) L1(all)

Ans. (i) (*b*) len() is used to calculate total occurrence of given element of list. L1 is a nested list which contains two sub-lists and a sub-list is considered as a single element.

(ii) (*c*) To print a specific range of elements from the list, we use slice operation. Slice operation is performed on lists with the use of colon (:). In L1[3 : 5], slicing start from index number 3, i.e. 'you' to index number (5 − 1) ⇒ 4 i.e. 'we'.

(iii) (*a*) To print elements from specific index till the end, use [Index:], so L1[5:] will print from index number 5 till end. i.e. 'those', 'these'. To print the element at specified index number use [index_number], so L1[2] will print the element at index number 2 which is a sub-list and considered as single element i.e. 'that', 'the', 'this'.
+ operator is used to concatenate the element of list.

(iv) (*b*) To print elements from specific index till the end, use [Index :], so L1[6:] will print from index number 6 till end i.e. "these".

(v) (*b*) To print the whole list, use [:], so L1[:] will print the entire list.

PART 2
Subjective Questions

• Short Answer Type Questions

1. What is nested list ? Explain with an example.

Ans. Nested lists are list objects where the elements in the lists can be lists themselves.
For example,
```
list1 = [45, 43, 12, 'Math', 'Eng', [75, 34,
                                    'A'], 5]
```
Here, list1 contains 7 elements, while inner list contains 3 elements. list1 is considered [75, 34, 'A'] as one element.

2.
```
list1 = [45, 77, 87, 'Next', 'Try', 33, 43]
```
Observe the given list and find the answer of questions that follows.
  (i) list1[-2]   (ii) list1[2]

Ans. (i) 33   (ii) 87

3. Distinguish between string and list.

Ans. Strings are immutable, which means the values provided to them will not change in the program. While lists are mutable which means the values of list can be changed at any point of time in program.

4. What is the output of below questions?
```
l2 = [75, 43, 40, 36, 28, 82]
```
  (i) l2.sort ( )
  (ii) l2.sort (reverse = True)

Ans. (i) [28, 36, 40, 43, 75, 82]
(ii) [82, 75, 43, 40, 36, 28]

5. Find the errors.
```
L1 = [2, 4, 5, 9]
L2 = L1 * 3
L3 = L1 + 3
L4 = L1. pop (5)
```

Ans. **Error 1** L3 = L1 + 3 because + operator cannot add list with other type as number or string.

Error 2 L1.pop (5) parentheses puts index value instead of element. In the given list, maximum index value is 3 and 5 is out of index range.

6. What will be the output of the following Python code?
```
a=[13,6,77]
a.append([87])
a.extend([45,67])
print(a)
```

Ans. [13,6,77, [87], 45, 67]

7. What will be the output of the following Python code?
```
a=[18,23,69,[73]]
b=list(a)
a[3][0]=110
a[1]=34
print(b)
```

Ans. [18, 23, 69, [110]]

8. Predict the output.
```
L2 = [4, 5, 3, 1]
L3 = [3, 4, 11, 2]
```
  (i) print (L2 + L3)
  (ii) print (L2. count (0))
  (iii) print (L3 [4])
  (iv) L3. remove (11)
     print (L3)

Ans. (i) [4, 5, 3, 1, 3, 4, 11, 2] (ii) 0
(iii) IndexError   (iv) [3, 4, 2]

9. Find the output.
```
L = [3, 4, 53, 4, 0, 2, 4, 7, 29]
(i) L [2 : 5]              (ii) L [: 7]
(iii) L [4 :]             (iv) [: : -1]
```
Ans. (i) [53, 4, 0]   (ii) [3, 4, 53, 4, 0, 2, 4]
(iii) [0, 2, 4, 7, 29]   (iv) [29, 7, 4, 2, 0, 4, 53, 4, 3]

10. Find the output of the given code.
```
list2 = ['A','R','I','H','A','N','T']
for i in range (len (list2)):
    print (list2 [i])
```
Ans. A
R
I
H
A
N
T

11. Define the replicating lists with an example.

Ans. In Python, you can repeat the elements of the list using (*) operator. This operator is used to replicate the list.
For example,
```
>>>l1 = [4, 5, 7, 1]
>>>l2 = l1 * 2
>>>l2
[4, 5, 7, 1, 4, 5, 7, 1]
```

12. Consider the following list and answer the below questions.
```
l1 = [89, 45, "Taj", "Qutub", 93, 42,
    "Minar", "Delhi", "Agra"]
(i) l1 [5 :]              (ii) "Qutab" not in l1
(iii) l1 [-3]             (iv) l1 [9]
(v) l1[2 : 5]             (vi) l1[-2 : 5]
```
Ans. (i) [42, 'Minar', 'Delhi', 'Agra']
(ii) False
(iii) 'Minar'
(iv) It gives IndexError because there is index value 0 to 8.
(v) ['Taj', 'Qutub', 93]
(vi) [ ]

13. Predict the output.
```
L1 = [3, 4, 5, 9, 11, 2, 27]
print (L1. index (3))
print (max (L1))
print (len (L1))
```
Ans. Output
0
27
7

14. Write the suitable method's name for the below conditions.

(i) Adds an element in the end of list.

(ii) Returns the index of first occurrence.

(iii) Adds contents of list2 to the end of list1.

Ans. (i) append ( )   (ii) index ( )
(iii) extend ( )

15. Consider the following list myList. What will be the elements of myList after the following two operations:
```
myList = [10,20,30,40]
(i) myList.append([50,60])
(ii) myList.extend([80,90])              [NCERT]
```
Ans. (i) [10, 20, 30, 40, [50, 60]]
(ii) [10, 20, 30, 40, 80, 90]

16. What will be the output of the following code segment?
```
myList = [1,2,3,4,5,6,7,8,9,10]
for i in range(0,len(myList)):
    if i%2 == 0:
        print(myList[i])              [NCERT]
```
Ans. 1
3
5
7
9

17. What will be the output of the following code segment?
```
(i) myList = [1,2,3,4,5,6,7,8,9,10]
    del myList[3:]
    print(myList)

(ii) myList = [1,2,3,4,5,6,7,8,9,10]
     del myList[:5]
     print(myList)

(iii) myList = [1,2,3,4,5,6,7,8,9,10]
      del myList[::2]
      print(myList)              [NCERT]
```
Ans. (i) [1, 2, 3]
(ii) [6, 7, 8, 9, 10]
(iii) [2, 4, 6, 8, 10]

18. Differentiate between append() and extend() functions of list.   [NCERT]

Ans. Differences between append() and extend() functions of list are

append()	extend()
append() method adds an element to a list.	extend() method concatenates the first list with another list (or another iterable).
When append() method adds its argument as a single element to the end of a list, the length of the list itself will increase by one.	extend() method iterates over its argument adding each element to the list, extending the list.

19. Consider a list:

```
list1 = [6,7,8,9]
```

What is the difference between the following operations on list1?

(i) `list1 * 2`

(ii) `list1 *= 2`

(iii) `list1 = list1 * 2` **[NCERT]**

Ans. (i) The statement will print the elements of the list twice, i.e. [6, 7, 8, 9, 6, 7, 8, 9]. However, list1 will not be altered.

(ii) This statement will change the list1 and assign the list with repeated elements, i.e. [6, 7, 8, 9, 6, 7, 8, 9] to list1.

(iii) This statement will also have same result as the statement 'list1 *= 2'. The list with repeated elements, i.e. [6, 7, 8, 9, 6, 7, 8, 9] will be assigned to list1.

20. What possible output(s) are expected to be displayed on screen at the time of execution of the program from the following code?

```
List = ["Poem", "Book", "Pencil", "Pen"]
List1 = List [2 : 3]
List[2] = "Scale"
print (List1)
```

Ans. ["Pencil"]

• Long Answer Type Questions

21. Write the best suited method's name for the following conditions.

(i) Insert an element at specified position.

(ii) Add contents from one list to other.

(iii) Calculate the total length of list.

(iv) Reverse the contents of the list object.

Ans. (i) insert ( )

(ii) extend ( )

(iii) len ( )

(iv) reverse ( )

22. Write a program to move all zeroes to the end of the list.

```
list1 = [4, 7, 0, 9, 8, 0, 2, 0, 4, 9, 0]
n = len (list1)
count = 0
for i in range (n):
    if list1[i] ! = 0:
        list1 [count] = list1[i]
        count + = 1
while count < n :
    list1 [count] = 0
    count + = 1
print ("List after pushing all zeroes to
                              end of list:")
print (list1)
```

Output

List after pushing all zeroes to end of list :

[4, 7, 9, 8, 2, 4, 9, 0, 0, 0, 0]

23. Observe the following list and answer the questions that follows.

```
l1 = [45, 65,"The", [65, "She", "He"],
90, 12, "This", 21]
```

(i) `l1 [3 : 4] = ["That", 54]`

(ii) `[l1 [4]]`

(iii) `l1 [:7]`

(iv) `l1 [1 : 2] + l1 [3 : 4]`

Ans. (i) [45, 65, 'The', 'That', 54, 90, 12, 'This', 21]

(ii) [54]

(iii) [45, 65, 'The', 'That', 54, 90, 12]

(iv) [65, 'That']

24. Write a Python program to find the third largest number in a entered list.

```
y = [ ]
num = int(input("Enter number of
elements:"))
for i in range (1, num + 1):
    x = int (input ("Enter element:"))
    y.append(x)
y. sort ()
print("Third largest element is :",
y[num-3])
```

Output

Enter number of elements : 5

Enter element : 76

Enter element : 45

Enter element : 98

Enter element : 90

Enter element : 23

Third largest element is : 76

25. Write Python program to display all the common elements of two lists.

```
list1 = [ ]
num = int (input ("Enter number of
elements in List1 :"))
for i in range (1, num +1):
    x = int (input("Enter element:"))
    list1. append (x)
list2 = [ ]
num1 = int (input ("Enter number of
elements in List2 :"))
for j in range (1, num1 +1):
    y = int (input ("Enter element:"))
    list2. append (y)
a_set = set (list1)
b_set = set (list2)
```

```
if (a_set & b_set):
    print ("Common elements are:", a_set &
    b_set)
else :
    print ("No common elements")
```

Output

```
Enter number of elements in List1:5
Enter element : 23
Enter element : –45
Enter element : 84
Enter element : –12
Enter element : 33
Enter number of elements in List2:5
Enter element : 12
Enter element : –45
Enter element : –65
Enter element : 41
Enter element : 32
Common elements are : {–45}
```

26. What will be the output of the following statements?

```
(i) list1 =  [12,32,65,26,80,10]
    list1.sort()
    print(list1)
(ii) list1 = [12,32,65,26,80,10]
    sorted(list1)
    print(list1)
(iii) list1 = [1,2,3,4,5,6,7,8,9,10]
    list1[::-2]
    list1[:3] + list1[3:]
(iv) list1 = [1,2,3,4,5]
    list1[len(list1)-1]                    [NCERT]
```

Ans. (i) [10, 12, 26, 32, 65, 80]
  (ii) [12, 32, 65, 26, 80, 10]
  (iii) [1, 2, 3, 4, 5, 6, 7, 8, 9, 10]
  (iv) 5

27. The record of a student (Name, Roll No., Marks in five subjects and percentage of marks) is stored in the following list:

```
stRecord =
['Raman','A-36',[56,98,99,72,69], 78.8]
```

Write Python statements to retrieve the following information from the list stRecord.

(i) Percentage of the student

(ii) Marks in the fifth subject

(iii) Maximum marks of the student

(iv) Roll No. of the student

(v) Change the name of the student from 'Raman' to 'Raghav'   [NCERT]

Ans. (i) `print(stRecord[3])`
  (ii) `print(stRecord[2][4])`
  (iii) `print(max(stRecord[2]))`
  (iv) `print(stRecord[1])`
  (v) `stRecord[0]='Raghav'`

28. Write a program to read a list of n integers (positive as well as negative). Create two new lists, one having all positive numbers and the other having all negative numbers from the given list. Print all three lists.   [NCERT]

Ans.
```
List = []
Pos = []
Neg = []
Num = int(input("Enter the Total Number
                 of List Elements : "))
for i in range(1, Num + 1):
    value = int(input("Enter the Value of
                      %d Element : " %i))
    List.append(value)
for j in range(Num):
    if(List[j] >= 0):
        Pos.append(List[j])
    else:
        Neg.append(List[j])
print("Element in Positive List is : ",
                                   Pos)
print("Element in Negative List is : ",
                                   Neg)
```

29. Write a program to read a list of n integers and find their median.

Note The median value of a list of values is the middle one when they are arranged in order. If there are two middle values then take their average.   [NCERT]

Hint You can use a built-in function to sort the list.

Ans.
```
num = int(input("Enter the number of
                 elements : "))
list1 = list()
for i in range(num):
    x = int(input("Enter the integer: "))
    list1.append(x)
print("Original list:",list1)
list1.sort()
print("Sorted list: ",list1)
c = len(list1)
if c%2 != 0:
    med = c//2
    print("Median: ",list1[med])
else:
    a = list1[c//2]
    b = list1[(c//2) - 1]
    s = a + b
```

```
med = s/2
print("Median: ", med)
```

30. Write a program to read a list of elements. Modify this list, so that it does not contain any duplicate elements, i.e. all elements occurring multiple times in the list should appear only once. **[NCERT]**

Ans.
```
list1=[]
num=int(input("Enter the number of
                       elements: "))
for i in range(num):
    x=int(input("Enter the element: "))
    list1.append(x)
print("New list: ")
print(list(set(list1)))
```

31. Write a program to read a list of elements. Input an element from the user that has to be inserted in the list. Also, input the position at which it is to be inserted. Write a user defined function to insert the element at the desired position in the list. **[NCERT]**

Ans.
```
num = int(input("Enter the number of
elements: "))
list1 = list()
for i in range(num):
    x = int(input("Enter the element: "))
    list1.append(x)
print("Original list: ",list1)
print()
pos = int(input("Enter the index
                      position: "))
ele = int(input("Enter the new element: "))
list1.insert(pos, ele)
print()
print("New list: ",list1)
```

32. Write a program to read elements of a list.

(i) The program should ask for the position of the element to be deleted from the list. Write a function to delete the element at the desired position in the list.

(ii) The program should ask for the value of the element to be deleted from the list. Write a function to delete the element of this value from the list. **[NCERT]**

Ans.
```
(i) num = int(input("Enter the number of
                        elements: "))
    list1 = list()
```
```
    for i in range(num):
        x = int(input("Enter the element:
                                "))
        list1.append(x)
    print("Original list: ",list1)
    print()
    pos = int(input("Enter the position of
    the element you want to delete: "))
    del list1[pos]
    print("List after deletion:",list1)
```
```
(ii) num = int(input("Enter the number of
     elements: "))
     list1 = list()
     for i in range(num):
         x = int(input("Enter the element:
                                 "))
         list1.append(x)
     print("Original list: ",list1)
     x = int(input("Enter the element you
                 want to delete: "))
     list1.remove(x)
     print("List after deletion: ",list1)
```

33. In Python, list is a type of container in data structures, which is used to store multiple data at the same time. It can store integer, string as well as object in a single list. Lists are mutable which means they can be changed after creation. Each element of a list is assigned a number its position or index. The first index is 0, the second index is 1, the third index is 2 and so on.

Based on the above information, answer the following questions.

(i) List is defined by which type of bracket?

(ii) List contains a sequence of what type of elements?

(iii) Lists are mutable. What is it mean?

(iv) Which method is also used to create list of characters and integers through keyboard?

(v) How to represent the first index of list?

Ans.
(i) []
(ii) Heterogeneous
(iii) Lists are mutable, which means they can be changed after creation
(iv) list ()
(v) 0

Chapter Test

Multiple Choice Questions

1. What is the output of following code?
```
list1=[4, 3, 7, 6, 4, 9, 5, 0, 3, 2]
l1=list1[1:10:3]
print(l1)
```
(a) [3, 7, 6]   (b) [3, 4, 0]
(c) [3, 6, 9]   (d) [7, 9,2]

2. Identify the output of following Python statement.
```
a = [[0, 1, 2], [3, 4, 5, 6]]
b = a [1] [2]
print (b)
```
(a) 2   (b) 1   (c) 4   (d) 5

3. Identify the output of following code.
```
list1 = [2, 3, 9, 12, 4]
list1.insert(4, 17)
list1.insert(2, 23)
print(list1 [-4])
```
(a) 4   (b) 9   (c) 12   (d) 23

4. What will be the output of the following Python code?
```
books = ['Hindi', 'English', 'Computer']
if 'put' in books:
    print(True)
else:
    print(False)
```
(a) True   (b) False   (c) None   (d) Error

5. Identify the output of the following Python statement.
```
list1=[4,3,7,9,15,0,3,2]
s = list1[2:5]
print(s)
```
(a) [7,9,15,0]   (b) [3,7,9,15]
(c) [7,9,15]   (d) [7,9,15,0,3]

6. What will be the output of following code?
```
list1=[2, 5, 4, [9, 6], 3]
list1[3][2] =10
print(list1)
```
(a) [2, 5, 4, [9, 10], 3]   (b) [2, 5, 4, 10, [9, 6], 3]
(c) Index out of range   (d) None of these

Short Answer Type Questions

7. What will be the output of the following Python code?
```
list1 = [11, 12, 13, 14, 15]
for i in range (1, 5) :
    list1[i-1] = list1[i]
for i in range (0, 5) :
    print(list1[i],end = " ")
```

8. What will be the output of following code?
```
l = []
for i in range (20, 40) :
    if(i % 7 == 0) and (i % 5! = 0) :
        l . append (str(i))
print ('.'. join(l))
```

9. What are the output of below questions?
```
L = [45, 89, 74, 12, 9, 83]
```
(i) L.remove ()
(ii) L.remove (12)

10. Predict the output.
```
L1 = [3, 2, 1]
L2 = [5, 9, 8]
```
(i) L1 * L2
(ii) L2.sort ( )
(iii) L1.reverse ( )

11. Write a program to input a list and print it in reverse order.

12. Give the output.
```
(i) str1 = 'aeiou'
   list1 = list(str1)
   print(list1)
(ii) list1 = [2, 3, 4, 5]
   list1. append(1)
   print(list1)
```

Long Answer Type Questions

13. Write the best suited method's name for the following conditions.
(i) Remove the value from the list.
(ii) Sort the elements in descending order.
(iii) Calculate the sum of all the elements of list.
(iv) Return the minimum element out of elements.

14. Write program to find the minimum and maximum elements from the entered list.

15. Write program to calculate the sum and mean of the elements which are entered by user.

16. Write program to count the frequency of elements in a list entered by user.

17. Write program to search for an element with its respective index number.

18. Write program to enter the elements of a list and reverse these elements.

Answers

Multiple Choice Questions

1. (b)   *2. (d)*   *3. (b)*   *4. (b)*   *5. (c)*   *6. (c)*

For Detailed Solutions
Scan the code

Tuples

In this Chapter...

A tuple is a collection of Python objects separated by commas (,) and put the elements in parentheses. Tuples are immutable by design which means they cannot be changed after creation. Tuple holds a sequence of heterogeneous elements. Tuples store a fixed set of elements and do not allow changes.

Tuple *vs* List

- Elements of a tuple are immutable whereas elements of a list are mutable.
- Tuples are declared in parentheses ( ), while lists are declared in square brackets [ ].
- Iterating over the elements of a tuple is faster compared to iterating over a list.

Creating a Tuple in Python

To create a tuple in Python, put all the elements in a parentheses ( ), separated by commas. We can have tuple of same type of data items as well as mixed type of data items.

```
a = (34, 76, 12, 90)
b = ('s', 3, 6, 'a')
c = (34, 0.5, 75)
d = ()
```

We can create different types of tuple in Python, which are as follows:

Empty Tuple

Empty tuple can be created in Python using ( ). It takes the truth value as false or equivalent of 0.

Here is the two ways to create empty tuple as

```
>>>t = ()
>>>print (t)
()
>>>t = tuple ()
>>>print(t)
()
```

Single Element Tuple

Creating a single element tuple is very complicated because it considered as integer value, if you give single element in a tuple.

```
>>>t=(8)
>>>t
8
>>>t=("a")
>>>t
'a'
```

For creating a single element tuple, you have to put comma (,) after the element.

```
>>>t = 8,
>>>t
(8,)
>>>t1 = (5,)
>>>t1
(5,)
>>>t2=("a",)
>>>t2
('a',)
```

Nested Tuple

Nested tuples are tuple objects where the elements in the tuples can be tuples themselves.

For example,
```
>>>t=(9, 6, 9, (1, 4, 8), 7)
>>>print(t)
(9, 6, 9, (1, 4, 8), 7)
```
It contains 5 elements while inner tuple contains 3 elements as (1, 4, 8). Tuple will considered (1, 4, 8) as one element.

Mixed Data Types Tuple

It can be created to place different data types such as integers, strings, double etc, into one tuple.

For example,
```
>>>t1=('Maths', 90, 89, 'English', 78.5)
>>>t1
('Maths', 90, 89, 'English', 78.5)
```

Creating Tuple from an Existing Sequence

In Python, tuple( ) method is used to create tuple from an existing sequence.

Syntax `new_tuple_name = tuple (sequence)`

Here is the sequence includes list, string, tuple etc.

For example,
```
>>>t="PROGRAM"
>>>t1=tuple(t)
>>>t1
('P', 'R', 'O', 'G', 'R', 'A', 'M')
>>>t=tuple("PROGRAM")
>>>t
('P', 'R', 'O', 'G', 'R', 'A', 'M')
>>>t1=['P', 'R', 'O', 'G', 'R', 'A', 'M']
>>>t2=tuple(t1)
>>>t2
('P', 'R', 'O', 'G', 'R', 'A', 'M')
```
tuple ( ) method is also used to create tuple of characters and integers which entered through keyboard.

For example,
```
>>>t=tuple (input("Enter the elements:"))
Enter the elements : 24567
>>>t
('2', '4', '5', '6', '7')
>>>b=tuple(input("Enter string :"))
Enter string : PUBLICATION
>>>b
('P', 'U', 'B', 'L', 'I', 'C', 'A', 'T', 'I', 'O', 'N')
```

Accessing Tuples

To access the tuple's elements, index number is used. Tuples are accessed similar of list except for the mutability. Use the index operator [ ], elements of a tuple can be access. The index should be an integer. Index of 0 refers to first element, 1 refers to second element and so on. While the index of −1 refers to the last element, −2 refers to the second last element and so on.

For example,
```
t1 = (87, 90, 'Maths', 'English', 56, 44, 99,
'Science', 23)
>>>t1[1]
90
>>>t1[− 2]
'Science'
>>>t1[7]
'Science'
>>>t1[4]
56
>>>t1[−3]
99
```

It is called positive index

0	1	2	3	4	5	6	7	8
87	90	'Maths'	'English'	56	44	99	'Science'	23
−9	−8	−7	−6	−5	−4	−3	−2	−1

It is called negative index

If we give index value out of range, then it will give error
```
>>>t1[9]
Trackback (most recent call last) :
File "<pyshell#8>", line 1, in <module>
    t1[9]
IndexError : tuple index out of range.
```
If you give index number with decimal point, it will also give error
```
>>>t1[4.5]
Trackback(most recent call last):
File"<pyshell#9>", line1, in <module>
    t1[4.5]
TypeError: tuple indices must be integers or
slices, not float.
```

Traversing a Tuple

Traversing a tuple is a technique to access an individual element of that tuple. It is also called iterate over a tuple.

There are multiple ways to iterate over a tuple in Python.

These are as follows:

Using for loop

The most common and easy way to traverse a tuple is with for loop. This method is used when you want to iterate all elements of a tuple.

Syntax `for variable in tuple_name :`

For example,
```
t=('P', 'Y', 'T', 'H', 'O', 'N')
for i in t :
    print(i)
```

Output
```
P
Y
T
H
O
N
```

Using for loop with range ( )

There is another method to traverse a tuple using for loop with range ( ). This is also used len() function with range.

This method is used when you want to iterate specified elements of a tuple.

Syntax `for index in range(len(tuple_name)):`

For example,
```
t=('P', 'Y', 'T', 'H', 'O', 'N')
for i in range (len(t)):
    print(t[i])
```

Output

P

Y

T

H

O

N

e.g. Program to display the elements of tuple ('A', 'R', 'I', 'H', 'A', 'N', 'T') in separate line with their index number.
```
tuple1=('A', 'R', 'I', 'H', 'A', 'N', 'T')
l=len(tuple1)
for i in range (l):
    print("Character:", tuple1[i],
        "at index number:", i)
```

Output

Character : A at index number : 0

Character : R at index number : 1

Character : I at index number : 2

Character : H at index number : 3

Character : A at index number : 4

Character : N at index number : 5

Character : T at index number : 6

Comparing Tuples

A comparison operator in Python is also called Python relational operator ($<$, $>$, $= =$, $! =$, $> =$, $< =$) that compares the values of two operands and returns True or False based on whether the condition is met.

Comparison operators for comparing tuples are as follows

Operators	Description	Example
Less than (<)	It checks if the left value is lesser than that on the right.	>>>a=(3, 5, 2, 7) >>>b=(3, 7, 0, 2) >>>a<b True
Greater than (>)	It checks if the left value is greater than that on the right.	>>>a=(4, 7, 2, 8) >>>b=(3, 7, (2), 8) >>>a>b True
Less than or Equal to (<=)	It returns True only if the value on the left is either less than or equal to that on the right of the operator.	>>>a=(0, 5, 1, 2) >>>b=(3, 4, 2, 5) >>>b<=a False

Operators	Description	Example
Greater than or Equal to (>=)	It returns True only if the value on the left is greater than or equal to that on the right of the operator.	>>>a=(4, 7, 2) >>>b=(2,(6,7), 4) >>>a>=b True
Equal to (= =)	It returns True if the values on either side of the operator are equal.	>>>a=(1,(2,3), 4) >>>b=(1,2,3,4) >>>a==b False
Not equal to (!=)	It returns True if the values on either side of the operator are unequal.	>>>a=(6, 7, 5) >>>b=(6, 4, 2) >>>a!=b True

Membership Operators

These operators are used to check whether a value/variable exists in the tuples. These operators return True or False as per the conditions met.

Membership operators in Python are two types as follows

in Operator

This operator is used to check if a value exists in a sequence or not. If it exists in the sequence, then it will return True else it will return False.

For example,
```
tuple1=(1,2,3,4,5)
tuple2=(6,7,8,9)
for item in tuple1:
    if item in tuple2:
        print("overlapping")
    else:
        print("not overlapping")
```

Output

not overlapping

not in Operator

This operator is the opposite of 'in' operator. So, if a value does not exist in the sequence then it will return a True else it will return a False.

For example,
```
x=44
y=30
tuple = (45, 65, 30, 78, 512)
if(x not in tuple):
    print("x is NOT present in given tuple")
else :
    print ("x is present in given tuple")
if(y in tuple):
    print("y is present in given tuple")
else:
    print("y is NOT present in given tuple")
```

Output

x is NOT present in given tuple

y is present in given tuple

Common Tuple Operations

We can perform various operations on tuple in Python. Some of them are describe below:

Concatenate Tuples

To concatenate tuples, (+) operator is used in Python. This operator can easily add the whole of one tuple to other tuple and perform concatenation.

For example,

```
>>>t1=(45, 65, 23, 9)
>>>t2=(34, 23, 65)
>>>t=t1+t2
>>>t
(45, 65, 23, 9, 34, 23, 65)
```

Concatenate operator (+) cannot add one tuple with other type as number or string. It will give error in such conditions.

For example,

```
>>>t1=(5, 3, 8, 3)
>>>t=t1+4
Trackback (most recent call last):
File "<pyshell # 5>", line1, in <module>
    t=t1+4
TypeError : can only concatenate tuple (not
"int") to tuple
>>>t1=(4,5,3)
>>>t = t1 + "Hello"
Trackback (most recent call last):
File "<pyshell#6>", line1, in <module>
    t = t1 + "Hello"
TypeError: can only concatenate tuple (not
"str") to tuple
```

Replicate Tuple

You can repeat the elements of the tuple using (*) operator. This operator is used to replicate the tuple.

For example,

```
>>>t1=(4, 6, 2, 8)
>>>t=t1*3
>>>t
(4, 6, 2, 8, 4, 6, 2, 8, 4, 6, 2, 8)
```

This operator cannot multiply two tuples.

```
>>>t1=(4, 5, 3)
>>>t2=(5, 0, 8)
>>>t=t1*t2
Trackback (most recent call last):
File "<pyshell#11>", line 1 , in <module>
    t=t1*t2
TypeError : can't multiply sequence by
non-int of type 'tuple'.
```

Tuple Slicing

In Python, there are multiple ways to display the tuple with all elements, but to display a specific range of elements from the tuple, we use slicing operation. This operation is performed on tuples with the use of colon (:).

Syntax `tuple_name [Start:Stop]`

For example,

```
>>>tuple1=(4, 7, 3, "This", 6, "That",
"These", 8, 9, "Those")
>>>t1=tuple1 [3:6]
>>>t1
('This', 6, 'That')
```

To display elements from beginning to a range use [: index], to display elements from end use [:-index] and to display elements from specific index till the end use [Index :]

For example,

```
>>>tuple1=(4, 7, 3, "This",
6,"That","These", 8,9,"Those")
>>>t2=tuple1[:6]
>>>t2
(4, 7, 3, 'This', 6, 'That')
>>>t3=tuple1[:-4]
>>>t3
(4, 7, 3, 'This', 6, 'That')
>>>t4=tuple1[-4:]
>>>t4
('These', 8, 9, 'Those')
>>>t5=tuple1[7:]
>>>t5
(8, 9, 'Those')
>>>t=(4,5,(3,7,5),9,2)
>>>t1=t[2:5]
>>>t1
((3, 7, 5), 9, 2)
>>>t2=t[4:-2]
>>>t2
()
```

We can also print all elements of tuple in reverse order using [::-1]

```
>>>t=tuple1[::-1]
>>>t
('Those', 9, 8, 'These', 'That', 6, 'This',
3, 7, 4)
>>>t=tuple1[2:-4]
>>>t
(3, 'This', 6, 'That')
```

Tuples are also provide slice steps which used to extract elements from tuple that are not consecutive.

Syntax `t=tuple_name[Start : Stop : Step]`

Here,

- **Start** integer where the slicing of the object starts.

- **Stop** integer until which the slicing takes place. The slicing stops at index stop-1.

- **Step** integer value which determines the increment between each index for slicing.

For example,
```
>>>t=(5, 3, "He","She", (4, 3,
"It"),3,"They", 8,9 "We")
>>>t1=t[2:8:2]
>>>t1
('He', (4, 3, 'It'), 'They')
>>>t2=t[::3]
>>>t2
(5, 'She', 'They', 'We')
>>>t3=t[6::]
>>>t3
("They", 8, 9, 'We')
```

Packing and Unpacking Tuples

In Python, tuples are collections of elements which are separated by commas. It packs elements or value together so, this is called packing. In other way, it is called unpacking of a tuple of values into a variable.

In packing, we put values together into a new tuple while in unpacking we extract those values into a single variables.

Syntax `variable1, variable2, ......, variableN = tuple_name`

For example,
```
>>>tuple1=(34, "Hello", 54, 89, "world")
```

To unpack the tuple, take variables equivalent to number of elements in that tuple and write this
```
>>>a, b, c, d, e = tuple1
```

Now, print individual variable which display the element of tuple.
```
>>>print(a)
34
>>>print(b)
Hello
>>>print(c)
54
>>>print(d)
89
>>>print(e)
world
```

Built-in Functions

In Python, tuple has large number of built-in functions which perform various operations and make the task easier. Some of them are describe below

(i) len()

This function is used to count the number of elements that present in the tuple.

Syntax `len(tuple_name)`

For example,
```
>>>t1=(45, "The", 67, 54, "That", 90)
>>>len(t1)
6
>>>t2=(45, "The", (67, 64), "That", 90)
>>>len(t2)
5
```

(ii) count()

This function is used to calculate total occurrence of given element of tuple.

Syntax `tuple_name.count(element)`

For example,
```
>>>t1=(10, 20, 30, 40, 10, 50, 20, 60, 10)
>>>t1.count(10)
3
>>>t1.count(20)
2
>>>t1.count(50)
1
>>>t1.count(90)
0
```

(iii) any( )

This function returns True if atleast one element is present in the tuple, otherwise returns False.

Syntax `any(tuple_name)`

For example,
```
>>>t1=(3, 6, 4)
>>>any(t1)
True
>>>t2=(2,)
>>>any (t2)
True
>>>t3=()
>>>any (t3)
False
```

(iv) max()

This function is used to return the element with maximum value out of elements present in tuple.

Syntax `max (tuple_name)`

For example,
```
>>>t1=(34, 65, 77, 45, 87, 99, 90)
>>>max (t1)
99
>>>t=(34, 65, "The")
>>>max(t)
Trackback (most recent call last):
File "<pyshell#5>", line 1, in <module>
   max(t)
TypeError : unorderable types : str( )>int( )
>>>t=('a', 'f', 'F', 'u')
>>>max(t)
'u'
```

It will return max value of character using ASCII value.

(v) min()

This function is used to return with minimum value out of elements present in tuple.

Syntax `min(tuple_name)`

For example,

```
>>>t1=(34, 65, 77, 45, 87, 99, 90)
>>>min(t1)
34
>>>t=('a', 'f','F', 'u')
>>>min(t)
'F'
>>>t2=("Ansh", "Yash", "Sahil")
>>>min(t2)
'Ansh'
```

(vi) sorted()

This function is used to sort the given tuple in ascending order. But this method returns the elements in square brackets.

Syntax `sorted(tuple_name)`

For example,

```
>>>t=(32, 45, 25, 33, 55, 89, 47, 78)
>>>sorted(t)
[25, 32, 33, 45, 47, 55, 78, 89]
>>>t1=('a', 'r', 'T', 'R', 'e', 'E')
>>>sorted(t1)
['E', 'R', 'T', 'a', 'e' , 'r']
```

(vii) index()

It returns the index of first occurrence of element in the tuple.

Syntax `tuple_name.index(element)`

For example,

```
>>>t=(45, 89, 9, "The", 23, "That", "This",
25)
>>>t.index('The')
3
>>>t.index(9)
2
>>>t.index(25)
7
>>>t.index("Those")
Trackback (most recent call last):
File "<pyshell#8>", line 1, in <module>
   t.index("Those")
ValueError : tuple.index(x) : x not in tuple.
```

(viii) tuple()

This function is used to convert string and list into tuple.

Syntax `tuple(list/string)`

For example,

```
>>>name="NIHARIKA"
>>>tuple(name)
('N', 'I', 'H', 'A', 'R', 'I', 'K', 'A')
```

```
>>>num = [4, 6, 3, 7, 2, 4, 0, 7]
>>>tuple (num)
(4, 6, 3, 7, 2, 4, 0, 7)
```

(ix) sum()

This method is used to calculate the sum of elements of tuple. The elements of tuple must be integer.

Syntax `sum(tuple_name)`

For example,

```
>>>marks=(78, 98, 80, 65, 75, 80)
>>>print ("Total marks :", sum(marks))
Total marks : 476
```

(x) reversed()

This method allows us to process the items in a sequence in reverse order. It accepts a sequence and returns an iterator.

Syntax `iterator = reversed (sequence)`

Here, sequence is a tuple.

For example,

```
>>>marks=(78, 98, 80, 65, 75, 80)
>>>t=reversed(marks)
>>>t
<reversed object at 0X00F49F70>
>>>for i in t:
   print(i)
80
75
65
80
98
78
```

or
```
>>>tuple(reversed (marks))
(80, 75, 65, 80, 98, 78)
```

Deleting a Tuple

Tuples are immutable and cannot be deleted individual element from it but deleting tuple entirely is possible by using the keyword "del".

For example,

```
t1=(4, 6, 3, 7, 6, 5, 0)
print("Tuple is :", t1)
del(t1)
print("Tuple after deletion")
print(t1)
```

Output

Tuple is : (4, 6, 3, 7, 6, 5, 0)

Tuple after deletion

Trackback (most recent call last) :

File "<pyshell#6>", line 1, in <module>
   print(t1)

NameError: name 't1' is not defined

Chapter Practice

Objective Questions

• Multiple Choice Questions

1. Which of the following is a collection of Python objects separated by commas and represent as (,)?
(a) List   (b) Tuple
(c) Dictionary   (d) String

Ans. (b) A tuple is a collection of Python objects separated by commas and represent as (,). Tuples are immutable by design which means they cannot be changed after creation. It holds a sequence of heterogeneous elements.

e.g. `T = (3, 4, 7, 6)`

2. What will be the output of the following Python code?

```
>>> a=(1,2,(4,5))
>>> b=(1,2,(3,4))
>>> a<b
```

(a) False
(b) True
(c) Error, < operator is not valid for tuples.
(d) Error, < operator is valid for tuples but not if there are sub-tuples.

Ans. (a) Since the first element in the sub-tuple of 'a' is larger that the first element in the sub-tuple of 'b', hence False is printed.

3. What is the output of the following code?

```
t1=(70, 56, 'Hello', 22, 2, 'Hi', 'The',
'World', 3)
print(t1 [2:4])
```

(a) (56, 'Hello')
(b) ('Hello', 22)
(c) ('Hello', 22,2)
(d) (56, 'Hello', 22)

Ans. (b) (:) is a slice operator, which returns the sub-part of any data type as string, list, tuple etc. Index number is started from 0, so the value of index number 2 is 'Hello' and this will display the elements till last index number − 1, i.e. (4 − 1=)3.
So, the correct output is ('Hello', 22).

4. Is the following Python code valid?

```
>>>tup1=(56, 25,36, 15)
>>> result=tup1.update(4,)
```

(a) Yes, tup1=(56, 25, 36, 15,4) and result=(56, 25, 36, 15,4)
(b) Yes, tup1=(56, 25, 36,15) and result=(56, 25, 36, 15,4)
(c) No, because tuples are immutable
(d) No, because wrong syntax for update() method

Ans. (c) Tuple does not have any update() attribute because it is immutable and cannot be changed after creation.

5. What is the output of following code?

```
t=(4,0, 'Hello', 90, 'Two', ('One', 45),
34, 2)
t1=t[1]+t[-2]
print(t1)
```

(a) 34   (b) 38
(c) Hello34   (d) 45

Ans. (a) Value of t[1] is 0 because index number is 1 and value of t[−2] is 34 because index number is started from −1 at the end point. t1 will store the sum of both values, i.e. 0+34=34.

6. What is the output of following code?

```
t=(1, 2, 'Hello', 'The', 3, 4)
print(max(t))
```

(a) 'Hello'   (b) 4
(c) 'The'   (d) Error

Ans. (d) This code will give an error because '>' (max) not supported between instances of 'str' and 'int'.

7. To create a tuple in Python, put all the elements in a
(a) ()   (b) []
(c) {}   (d) <>

Ans. (a) To create a tuple in Python, put all the elements in a parentheses (), separated by commas. We can have tuple of same type of data items as well as mixed type of data items.

```
>>> t = ()
>>> print(t)
()
```

8. Suppose `t1 = (3, 4, 5,8, 2, 1)`
Find the value of t1[3.5].
(a) 8   (b) 2
(c) 5   (d) Error

And. (d) It will give TypeError because tuple's index must be integers or slices, not float.

9. Suppose tuple `t1 = (3, 4, 5, 6, 7, 8)`
Choose the correct option for t1[6].
(a) 1   (b) 8
(c) None   (d) Error

Ans. (d) It will give IndexError because tuple index is out of range. Its maximum index is 5 because index is started from 0 but in t1[6] asked about index number 6, so it will give an error.

10. Tuple packs elements or value together, so this is called
(a) pickling   (b) unpacking
(c) packing   (d) unpickling

Ans. (c) Tuple packs elements or value together, so this is called packing. In packing, we put values together into a new tuple while in unpacking we extract those values into a single variable.

11. Choose the correct output.
```
a = (2, 4, 3, 4)
b = (5, 8, 9)
t = a + b
print(t)
```
(a) (2, 4, 3, 4, 5, 8, 9)   (b) (7, 12, 12, 4)
(c) (2, 10, 13, 4, 9)   (d) Error

Ans. (a) To concatenate tuples, (+) operator is used in Python. This operator can easily add the whole of one tuple to other tuple and perform concatenation. This operator cannot add one tuple with other type as number or string, otherwise it will give error in such conditions.

12. Suppose tuple `t1 = (4, 7, 3, 6, 8, 9)`

Choose the correct option for t1[: 4].
(a) (3, 6, 8, 9)   (b) (4, 7, 3, 6)
(c) (6)   (d) (8, 9)

Ans. (b) To display a specific range of elements from the tuple, we use slicing operation. This operation in performed on tuples with the use of colon (:).
To display elements from beginning to a range, use [: index].
So, t1[: 4] will print the element from starting to index−1.

13. Given a tuple t1= (1, 2, 3, 4, 5, 6, 7, 8, 9). What will be the output of print (t1 [3 : 7 : 2])?
(a) (4, 5, 6, 7, 8)   (b) (4, 5, 6, 7)
(c) (4, 5, 6)   (d) (4, 6)

Ans. (d) `t1[3 : 7 : 2]` starts from index number 3 to index number 7 with gap of 2 elements.
In t1= (1, 2, 3, 4, 5, 6, 7, 8, 9), element of index number 3 is 4 and after two elements of gap, element is 6. So, output is (4, 6).

14. Given a tuple t1= (1, 2, 3, 4, 5). Identify the statement that will display an error.
(a) `print (t1[3])`
(b) `t1[4] = 7`
(c) `print (len (t1))`
(d) `print (max (t1))`

Ans. (b) t1[4] = 7 means updation which is not possible in tuple because tuple is immutable which cannot be changed after creation.

15. What is the output of following code?
```
T = (100)
print (T * 2)
```
(a) Syntax error   (b) (200,)
(c) 200   (d) (100, 100)

Ans. (c) Tuple T contains a single element, so * is used as multiplication operator.
So, T * 2 = 100 * 2 = 200

16. What will be the output of the following Python code?
```
>>> a=(5,6)
>>> b=(2,6)
>>> c=a+b
>>> c
```
(a) (7,12)
(b) (5,6,2,6)
(c) Error as tuples are immutable
(d) None

Ans. (b) In the above piece of code, the values of the tuples are not being changed. Both the tuples are simply concatenated.

17. Choose the correct option.
(a) In Python, a tuple can contain only integers as its elements.
(b) In Python, a tuple can contain only strings as its elements.
(c) In Python, a tuple can contain both integers and strings as its elements.
(d) In Python, a tuple can contain either string or integer but not both at a time.

Ans. (c) In Python, a tuple can contain both integers and strings as its elements is the correct option.

• Case Based MCQs

18. Suppose that tuple
```
t1=("Hello", ("am", "an"), ("that", "the",
"this"), "you", "we", "those", "these")
```
Based on the above information, answer the following questions.

(i) Choose the correct option for len(t1).
(a) 7   (b) 10
(c) None   (d) Error

(ii) What is the output of following code?
```
print(t1[3 :5])
```
(a) ('the', 'this')   (b) ('am', 'an')
(c) ('you', 'we')   (d) ('you', 'we', 'those')

(iii) Identify the output of t1[5 :] + t1[2].
(a) ('those', 'these', 'that')
(b) ('those', 'these', 'that', 'the', 'this')
(c) ('the', 'this')
(d) Error

(iv) Identify the output of print (t1[6:]).
   (a) ('these',)
   (b) ('those')
   (c) 'these'
   (d) Error

(v) Find the correct output of print (t1[−3]*2).
   (a) wewe
   (b) youyou
   (c) None
   (d) IndexError

Ans. (i) (a) len() is used to count the number of elements that present in the tuple. Given tuple is a nested tuple, so ("am", "an") will considered as one element and ("that", "the", "this") will considered as one element. Then, this will give 7 as output.

(ii) (c) To display a specific range of elements from the tuple, we use slicing operation. This operation is performed on tuples with the use of colon (:).

t1[3 : 5] displays the element from index number 3, i.e. 'you' to index number (5 −1 =) 4 i.e. we. So, output will be ('you', 'we').

(iii) (b) To display elements from specific index till the end, use [index :], so t1[5:] will display the elements from index number 5 to till end i.e. ('those', 'these').

To access a particular element, use [index], so t1[2] will display the element of index number 2, i.e. ('that', 'the', 'this').

+ operator is used to concatenate the tuples.

(iv) (a) To display elements from specific index till the end, use [Index :].

So, t1[6:] will display the element from index number 6, i.e. 'these' till the end.

(v) (a) Index number − 3 represents the third element from end i.e. 'we'. * is the replication operator that can repeat the elements of the tuple.

So, 'we' will be repeat two times because * 2 is given.

PART 2
Subjective Questions

• Short Answer Type Questions

1. Distinguish between tuple and list.

Ans. Differences between tuple and list are as follows

Tuple	List
Elements of a tuple are immutable.	Elements of a list are mutable.
Tuple is declared in parenthesis ().	List is declared in square brackets [ ].
Tuples cannot be changed after creation.	Lists can be changed after creation.
Iterating over the elements of a tuple is fast.	Iterating over the elements of a list is slow.

2. Explain the mixed data types tuple with an example.

Ans. Mixed data types can be created to place different data types such as integers, strings, double etc into one tuple. *For example,*
```
tuple1=('English', 90, 'Rahul','Meerut','99.5')
```

3. Observe the following tuple and answer the questions that follow.
```
t1=(76, 56, 'Harish', 'Ansh', 98, (45, 34),'Muskan')
```
(i) len(t1)   (ii) t1[−6]
(iii) t1[3]   (iv) t1[: 2]

Ans. (i) 7
(ii) 56
(iii) 'Ansh'
(iv) (76, 56)

4. Explain sum() method of tuple with an example.

Ans. sum() method is used to calculate the sum of elements of tuple. The elements of tuple must be integer.

Syntax sum(tuple_name)

For example,
```
>>>price=(100, 150, 95, 120, 80)
>>>sum(price)
```
Output
```
545
```

5. Observe the following tuples and answer the questions that follow.
```
t1=(4, 7, 8, 9)
t2=(0, 4, 3)
```
(i) >>>t=t1+t2
   >>>print(t)
(ii) >>>t=t1*t2
   >>>print(t)

Ans. (i) (4, 7, 8, 9, 0, 4, 3)
(ii) It gives TypeError because cannot multiply sequence by non-int of type 'tuple'.

6. Write a Python program to find maximum and minimum elements in a tuple.

Ans.
```
tuple1 = (23,45,−65,−45,20,45,65,− 24)
print("The tuple is:",tuple1)
min1 = tuple1.index (min(tuple1))
max1 = tuple1.index (max(tuple1))
print("Maximum element in the tuple is :",
max(tuple1)," at index number ",max1)
print("Minimum element in the tuple is :",
min(tuple1)," at index number ",min1)
```

7. What do you mean by membership operators in Python?

Ans. Membership operators are used to check whether a value/variable exists in the sequence like string, list, tuple etc. These operators return True or False as per conditions met.

Membership operators are of two types as:

  (i) in operator

  (ii) not in operator

8. Explain tuple slicing syntax with its parameters.

Ans. Syntax `t=tuple_name[start : stop : step]`

Here,

- **start** integer where the slicing of the object starts.
- **stop** integer until which the slicing takes place. The slicing stops at index stop−1.
- **step** integer value which determines the increment between each index for slicing.

9. Find the output of the given questions

```
t=(45, 76, 23, 'The', 89, ('This', 56), (23,
'That'),34)
```

  (i) `(t[4])`

  (ii) `t[2:10:3]`

  (iii) `t[2] + t [-1]`

Ans. (i) 89

  (ii) (23,('This', 56))

  (iii) 57

10. Find the output of following code?

```
t = ('A', 'R', 'I', 'H', 'A', 'N', 'T')
for i in range (len(t)):
        print (t[i])
```

Ans. Output

  A

  R

  I

  H

  A

  N

  T

11. What will be the output of following code?

```
tuple1=(1,2,3,4,5)
tuple2=(6,7,8,9)
for item in tuple1:
    if item in tuple2:
        print("overlapping")
    else:
        print("not overlapping")
```

Ans. Output

not overlapping

12. What will be the output of following code?

```
x=44
y=30
tuple = (45, 65, 30, 78, 512)
if(x not in tuple):
    print("x is NOT present in given tuple")
```

```
else :
    print ("x is present in given tuple")
if(y in tuple):
    print("y is present in given tuple")
else:
    print("y is NOT present in given tuple")
```

Ans. x is NOT present in given tuple

y is present in given tuple

13. What is the output of following code?

```
t1=(1, 2, 3, 4, 5)
print("Tuple is :", t1)
del(t1)
print("Tuple after deleting")
print(t1)
```

Ans. Output

Tuple is : (1, 2, 3, 4, 5)

Tuple after deleting

Trackback (most recent call last) :

File "<pyshell#6>", line 1, in <module>

    print(t1)

NameError: name 't1' is not defined

14. Find and write the output of the following Python code.

```
t=(4, (8, 0, 7))
t1=(4, 7, (2, 8))
print(t.count(0))
print(t[1][2])
print(t*2)
print(len(t1))
print(t1[2])
print(t+t1)
```

Ans. Output

  0

  7

  (4, (8, 0, 7), 4, (8, 0, 7))

  3

  (2, 8)

  (4, (8, 0, 7), 4, 7, (2, 8))

15. Identify the error, if any in the following code.

```
t1=(2, 3, 4, 'Hello', 6,9)
print (min(t1))
```

Ans. min() function is used in tuple to return with minimum value out of elements in tuple.

Given code has an error because min() will work only if elements in a tuple are of same data type, i.e. (2, 3, 4, 7, 6, 9).

16. Write a Python code to remove an element '2' from the following tuple.

```
tuple1 = (2, 5, 6, 9, 4)
```

Ans.
```
tuple1 = (2, 5, 6, 9, 4)
list1 = list (tuple1)
list1. remove (2)
tuple1 = tuple (list1)
print (tuple1)
```

17. Write a Python code to display all the elements of the following tuple except 'H'.

```
t = ('A', 'R', 'I', 'H', 'A', 'N', 'T')
```

Ans.
```
t = ('A', 'R', 'I', 'H', 'A', 'N', 'T')
t = t[0 : 3] + t[-3 : ]
print (t)
```
Output
```
('A', 'R', 'I', 'A', 'N', 'T')
```

18. TypeError occurs while statement 2 is running. Give reason. How can it be corrected?

```
>>> tuple1 = (5) #statement 1
>>> len(tuple1) #statement 2
```
[NCERT]

Ans. The 'statement 1' is creating a variable, tuple1 which is of 'int' data type. The 'statement 2' is checking for the length of the variable, but the argument passed is an 'int' data type. The len() function can return the length only when the object is a sequence or a collection. This is the reason for the type error.

The error can be corrected by adding one comma after '5' in statement 1, as this will create a tuple and as a tuple is a collection, len() function will not return an error.

The correct statement will be
```
>>> tuple1 = (5,)
>>> len(tuple1)
```

19. Prove with the help of an example that the variable is rebuilt in case of immutable data types. [NCERT]

Ans. When a variable is assigned to the immutable data type, the value of the variable cannot be changed in place.

Therefore, if we assign any other value of the variable, the interpreter creates a new memory location for that value and then points the variable to the new memory location. This is the same process in which we create a new variable. Thus, it can be said that the variable is rebuilt in case of immutable data types on every assignment.

Program to represent the same:
```
v = 20
print("Before: ",id(v))
v = 21
print("After: ",id(v))
```
Output

Before: 140705582623120

After: 140705582623152

It can be seen that the memory location a variable is pointing after the assignment is different. The variable is entirely new and it can be said that the variable is rebuilt.

• Long Answer Type Questions

20. Write the short note on following terms.

(i) Tuple

(ii) in operator

(iii) Equal to (= =) operator

(iv) Packing

Ans. (i) Tuple is a collection of Python objects separated by commas (,) and put the elements in parentheses ( ).

(ii) in operator is used to check, if a value exists in a sequence.

(iii) Equal to (= =) operator returns True if the values on either side of the operator are equal.

(iv) Tuples put all the elements or values together in a parentheses, is called packing.

21. Answer the following questions;

(i)
```
t1=(25, 78, (45, (65, 89)), 90, (34, 8))
len (t1)
```

(ii)
```
t2=(45,('The',78,('This'),67),'The',67, 67)
t2.count(67)
```

(iii)
```
t1=(3,)
t2=()
t=t1+t2
any(t)
```

(iv)
```
t3=(87, 89, 56, 99, 75, 45, 100)
max(t3)
```

Ans. (i) 5   (ii) 2   (iii) True   (iv) 100

22. Write a Python program to count the number of elements in a given range using traversal. Also, display its output.

Ans.
```
c=0
l=40
r=80
tuple1=(10, 20, 30, 40, 50, 40, 40, 60, 70)
for x in tuple1:
    if x>=l and x<=r:
        c+=1
print("Tuple:", tuple1)
print("Elements in a tuple:",c)
```

Output

Tuple : (10, 20, 30, 40, 50, 40, 40, 60, 70)

Elements in a tuple : 6

23. Write a Python program to find the common elements in two tuples.

Ans.
```
tuple1=(45,87,56,-78,36,-12)
tuple2=(65,32,45,-78,36,-75)
a_set = set(tuple1)
b_set = set(tuple2)
if (a_set & b_set):
    print("Common elements are:",a_set &
    b_set)
else:
    print("No common elements")
```

Output

Common elements are: {-78, 36, 45}

24. Write a Python program to calculate the sum and mean of the elements in a tuple.

Ans.
```
tuple1 = (23,45,20,45,65,24)
print("The tuple is:",tuple1)
sm=0
for i in range(len(tuple1)):
    sm=sm+tuple1[i]
mean=sm/num
print("SUM = ",sm)
print("MEAN = ",mean)
```
Output
The tuple is: (23, 45, 20, 45, 65, 24)
SUM = 222
MEAN = 44.4

25. Write a program to find the occurrence of a given element.

Ans.
```
t = (23,45,20,-45,65,24,-45,-23)
print("The tuple is:",t)
k=0
num=int(input("Enter the number to be
                         counted:"))
for j in t:
    if(j==num):
        k=k+1
print("Number",num,"is appear",k, "times.")
```
Output
The tuple is: (23, 45, 20, − 45, 65, 24, − 45, − 23)
Enter the number to be counted:45
Number 45 is appear 1 times.

26. Write a Python program to search an element with its index number.

Ans.
```
tuple1=(12,65,78,-63,-2,3,78,-12)
sm=0
x = int(input("Enter number to be searched:"))
found = False
for i in range(len(tuple1)):
    if(tuple1[i] == x):
        found = True
        print("%d found at %drd
                         position"%(x,i))
        break
if(found == False):
    print("%d is not in tuple"%x)
```
Output
Enter number to be searched: − 63
− 63 found at 3rd position

27. Consider the following tuples, tuple1 and tuple2.
```
tuple1 = (23,1,45,67,45,9,55,45)
tuple2 = (100,200)
```

Find the output of the following statements.
(i) `print(tuple1.index(45))`
(ii) `print(tuple1.count(45))`
(iii) `print(tuple1 + tuple2)`
(iv) `print(len(tuple2))`
(v) `print(max(tuple1))`
(vi) `print(min(tuple1))`
(vii) `print(sum(tuple2))`
(viii) `print(sorted(tuple1))`
    `print(tuple1)`   **[NCERT]**

Ans. (i) 2
(ii) 3
(iii) (23, 1,45, 67,45, 9, 55, 45, 100, 200)
(iv) 2
(v) 67
(vi) 1
(vii) 300
(viii) [1, 9, 23, 45, 45, 45, 55, 67]
(23,1,45,67,45,9,55,45)

28. Write a program to read email IDs of n number of students and store them in a tuple. Create two new tuples, one to store only the usernames from the email IDs and second to store domain names from the email IDs. Print all three tuples at the end of the program.

[**Hint** You may use the function split()]   **[NCERT]**

Ans.
```
num = int(input("Enter number of students: "))
list1=[]
for i in range(num):
    email=input("Enter email: ")
    list1.append(email)
tuple1=tuple(list1)
username=[]
domain=[]
for i in tuple1:
    n,d = i.split("@")
    username.append(n)
    domain.append(d)
username = tuple(username)
domain = tuple(domain)
print("Names = ",username)
print("Domains = ",domain)
print("Tuple = ",tuple1)
```

29. A tuple is a collection of objects which ordered and immutable. Tuples are sequences, just like lists. The differences between tuples and lists are, the tuples cannot be changed unlike lists and tuples use parentheses, whereas lists use square brackets. We can use the index operator [] to access an item in a tuple, where the index starts from 0.

So, a tuple having 6 elements will have indices from 0 to 5. Trying to access an index outside of the tuple index range(6,7,... in this example) will raise an IndexError.

(i) Which types of elements are stored in tuple?

(ii) What do you mean by nested tuples?

(iii) Write the syntax to create tuple from an existing sequence.

(iv) Observe the output of giving code.

```
>>>t=["T", "U", "P", "L", "E"]
>>>t2 = tuple(t)
>>>t2
```

(v) What is traversing a tuple in Python?

Ans. (i) Tuples hold a sequence of heterogeneous elements.

(ii) Nested tuples are tuple objects where the elements in the tuples can be tuples themselves.

(iii) `new_tuple_name=tuple(sequence)`

(iv) ('T', 'U', 'P', 'L', 'E')

(v) Traversing a tuple is a technique to access an individual element of that tuple.

Chapter Test

Multiple Choice Questons

1. Consider the declaration obj = (2, 'Hello', 3, 4). What will be the data type of obj?
   (a) List
   (b) Tuple
   (c) Dictionary
   (d) String

2. What is the output of followig code?
```
t1=(1, 2, 3, 4, 5, 6, 7, 8)
print (t1[2 : 4])
```
   (a) (3, 4)
   (b) (2, 3)
   (c) (4, 5, 6)
   (d) (3, 4, 5)

3. Choose the correct option with respect to Python.
   (a) Both tuples and lists are immutable.
   (b) Tuples are immutable while lists are mutable.
   (c) Both tuples and lists are mutable.
   (d) Tuples are mutable while lists are immutable.

4. Which of the following options will not result in an error when performed on tuples in Python where tupl=(5,2,7,0,3)?
   (a) tupl[1]=2
   (b) tupl.append(2)
   (c) tupl1=tupl+tupl
   (d) tupl.sort()

5. What will be the output of the following Python code?
```
>>>my_tuple = (10, 20, 30, 40)
>>>my_tuple.append((50, 60))
>>>print (len(my_tuple))
```
   (a) 1
   (b) 6
   (c) 4
   (d) Error

6. Is the following Python code valid?
```
>>> a,b=1,2,3
```
   (a) Yes, this is an example of tuple unpacking, where a=1 and b=2.
   (b) Yes, this is an example of tuple unpacking, where a=(1,2) and b=3.
   (c) No, too many values to unpack.
   (d) Yes, this is an example of tuple unpacking, where a=1 and b=(2,3).

Short Answer Type Questions

7. Observe the following tuple and answer the questions that follow
```
t = (1, 2, 3, 4, 5,6 ,7,8, 9,10)
```
   (i) t[−3]
   (ii) t[: 2]

8. Explain the any () method of tuple with an example.

9. Suppose the tuple t1 = (2, 3, 4, 7, 1, 6). Find
   (i) `t1.index(4)`
   (ii) `t1.count(4)`

10. Suppose the tuple t1 = (2, 3, 2, 2, 3, 4, 6, 7).
   (i) `count (t1)`
   (ii) `len(t1)`

11. Observe the given tuples and answers the questions
```
t1 = (1, 2, 3, 4)
t2 = (5, 6, 7)
```
   (i) `>>> t = t1 + t2`
   `   >>> print(t)`
   (ii) `>>> t = t1 * t2`
   `   >>> print(t)`

12. Consider the tuple t = (2,3, 'Hello', 2, 5, 9) and find out the error if any in following code
```
tuple1 = t + 5
print(tuple1)
```

13. Compare the tuple and write the output.
   (i)
```
t1 = (4, 5, 6, 9)
t2 = (6, 9, 5, 6)
print(t1 < t2)
```
   (ii)
```
t1 = (4, 5, 6, 9)
t2 = (4.0, 5.0, 6.0, 9.0)
print(t1 == t2)
```

Long Answer Type Questions

14. Write a Python program to count the positive numbers and negative numbers in a tuple.

15. Write the most appropriate tuple methods for the following conditions.
   (i) To count the number of elements in a tuple.
   (ii) Calculate total occurence of given element.
   (iii) Returns the element with maximum value.
   (iv) Returns the element with minimum value.
   (v) To sort the given tuple in ascending order.
   (vi) Returns true if atleast one element is present in the tuple.
   (vii) Returns the index of first occurrence of element.
   (viii) Converts string and list into tuple.

16. Write a Python program to test if a variable is a list or tuple.

17. Write a Python program to sort a list of tuples by the second Item.

18. Write a Python program to sort a list of tuples alphabetically.

Answers

Multiple Choice Questions

   1. (b)   2. (a)   3. (b)   4. (c)   5. (d)   6. (c)

For Detailed Solutions
Scan the code

Dictionary

In this Chapter...

- Creating a Dictionary
- Properties of Dictionary Keys
- Traversing a Dictionary
- Accessing Keys or Values Separately
- Adding Elements to Dictionary
- Updating Elements in a Dictionary
- Deleting Element from a Dictionary
- Membership Operators
- Built-in Methods

In Python, dictionary is an unordered collection of data values that stored the key : value pair instead of single value as an element. Keys of a dictionary must be unique and of immutable data types such as strings, tuples etc. Immutable means they cannot be changed after creation. But in dictionary, key-value can be repeated and be of any type.

A dictionary is used to map or associate things you want to store the keys you need to get them. A dictionary in Python is just like a dictionary in the real world. Each key-value pair in a dictionary is separated by a colon (:) whereas each key is separated by a comma (,). In dictionary, key will be a single element and values can be a list or list within a list, numbers etc.

Creating a Dictionary

To create a dictionary in Python key : value pair is used. Dictionary is listed in curly brackets, inside these curly brackets, keys and values are declared.

Syntax `dictionary_name = {key1 : value1, key2 : value2, …}`

For example,

```
>>>Employees = {"Abhi" : "Manager", "Manish" :
"Project Manager", "Aasha" : "Analyst",
"Deepak" : "Programmer", "Ishika" : "Tester"}
>>> Employees
```

Here is the example of dictionary named Employees in which Emplyees' names stored as keys and designation stored as values of respected keys.

Output

{'Abhi': 'Manager', 'Manish' : 'Project Manager', 'Aasha' : 'Analyst', 'Deepak' : 'Programmer', 'Ishika' : 'Tester'}

We can separate these dictionaries as follows

Key : Value Pair	Key	Value
"Abhi" : "Manager"	"Abhi"	"Manager"
"Manish" : "Project Manager"	"Manish"	"Project Manager"
"Aasha" : "Analyst"	"Aasha"	"Analyst"
"Deepak" : "Programmer"	"Deepak"	"Programmer"
"Ishika" : "Tester"	"Ishika"	"Tester"

We can also create empty dictionary.

For example, `dic1 = { }`

Dictionaries are also called **mappings** or **hashes** or **associative arrays**.

If you give list as key, then it will give an Error

```
>>> dic = {[1, 2]: "math"}
Trackback (most recent call last):
    File "<pyshell#7>", line 1, in <module>
        dic = {[1, 2]: "math"}
TypeError : unhashable type : 'list'
```

Properties of Dictionary Keys

There are following points while using dictionary keys as follows

(i) More than one entry per key is not allowed (no duplicate key is allowed).

(ii) Dictionaries' keys are case sensitive, same key name but with the different case are treated as different in Python.

(iii) The values in the dictionary can be of any type while the keys must be immutable like numbers, tuples or strings.

Accessing Elements from a Dictionary

In Python, to access the elements from a dictionary, keys are used. While in tuple and list, index is used to access the elements.

Syntax `dictionary_name[key]`

To access the respective value of key, that key has to given in square bracket with dictionary name.

For example,

```
>>>Employees ["Deepak"]
'Programmer'
>>>Employees ["Ishika"]
'Tester'
```

You can also give this as

```
>>>print ("Manish works as a", Employees
['Manish'])
Manish works as a Project Manager
```

If you give a key that does not exist in dictionary, then it will give an error. So, before to access the value first ensure that key is available in dictionary or not.

```
>>>Employees ["Tushar"]
Trackback (most recent call last):
    File "<pyshell#11>", line1, in <module>
    Employees ["Tushar"]
KeyError : 'Tushar'
```

If you do not give any key with dictionary name, then it will give whole dictionary with different order.

For example,

```
>>>dic = {'1' : "Math", '2' : "Science", '3' :
"English"}
>>>dic
{'1' : 'Math', '3' : 'English', '2' :
'Science'}
```

Traversing a Dictionary

Traversing a dictionary means access each and every element of it. We can traverse a dictionary using for loop.

For example,

```
dic = {1 : "Math", 2 : "Science", 3 : "English"
4 : "Music"}
```

There are multiple ways to iterate over (traversing) a dictionary in Python as follows

(i) Iterate Through All Keys

In above example, the order of subject number will change every time because the dictionary does not store keys in a particular order.

```
>>>print ("Keys are")
>>>for i in dic :
        print(i)
```

Output

```
Keys are
1
2
3
4
```

(ii) Iterate Through All Values

Again, in above example, the order of subjects are printed will change every time.

For example,

```
>>>print ("Values are")
>>>for i in dic:
        print(dic [i])
```

Output

```
Values are
Math
Science
English
Music
```

(iii) Iterate Through All Keys Value Pairs

We can also iterate dictionary through all keys value pairs.

For example,

```
>>>print ("Keys :Values")
>>>for i in dic :
        print(i, ":", dic [i])
```

Output

```
Keys : Values
1 : Math
2 : Science
3 : English
4 : Music
```

Accessing Keys or Values Separately

You can access the keys or values separately in dictionary. To access the keys from dictionary, use `(dictionary_name). keys ()` and to access the values of respected keys, use `(dictionary_name). values ()`

For example,

```
>>>dic1 = {"A" : "Science", "B" : "Math", "C" :
"Computer", "D" : "English"}
>>>dic1.keys ()
dict_keys (['B', 'C', 'A', 'D'])
>>>dic1.values ()
dict_values (['Math', 'Computer', 'Science',
'English'])
```

You can also convert these returned keys and values in list form.

For example,
```
>>>list (dic1.keys())
['B', 'C', 'A', 'D']
>>list (dic1.values ())
['Math', 'Computer', 'Science', 'English']
```

Nested Dictionary

Nested dictionary means putting a dictionary inside another dictionary. Nesting is of great use as kind of information we can model in programs expanded greatly.

Syntax
```
Nested_dict = {'dictA' : {'key1' : 'value1'},
'dictB' : {'key2' : 'value2'}}
```

Here, the Nested_dict is a nested dictionary with the dictionary dictA and dictB. They are two dictionaries and each having own key and value.

For example,
```
>>>Student = {112 : {'Name' : 'Surbhi',
'Marks' : 450, 'Age' : 16}, 115 : {'Name' :
'Sahil', 'Marks' : 470, 'Age' : 16}}
>>>Student
{112 : {'Marks' : 450, 'Age' : 16, 'Name' :
'Surbhi'},
115 : {'Marks' : 470, 'Age' : 16, 'Name' :
'Sahil'}}
```

Adding Elements to Dictionary

In Python dictionary, adding of elements extend it with single pair of values. One value at a time can be added to a dictionary by defining value along with the key.

Syntax
```
dictionary_name [key] = value
```

For example,
```
>>>Teacher = {'Neha' : 'Hindi', 'Akshay' :
'Math', 'Parul' : 'English'}
>>>Teacher ['Nisha'] = 'Computer'
>>>Teacher
{'Akshay' : 'Math', 'Nisha' : 'Computer' ,
'Neha' : 'Hindi', 'Parul' : English'}
```

You can also adding elements into an empty dictionary by dictionary_name [key] = value
```
>>>dic = { }
>>>dic
{ }
>>>dic [1] = "Delhi"
>>>dic [2] = "Meerut"
>>>dic [3] = "Agra"
>>>dic [4] = "Chandigarh"
>>>dic
{1 : 'Delhi', 2 : 'Meerut', 3 : 'Agra', 4 :
'Chandigarh'}
```

Updating Elements in a Dictionary

You can update elements that are already exist in a dictionary.

Syntax
```
dictionary_name [key] = value
```

For example,
```
>>>Student = {11 : 'Ashi', 12 : 'Shivam', 13 :
'Shrey', 14 : 'Vicky'}
>>>Student [12] = 'Nishant'
>>>Student
{11 : 'Ashi', 12 : 'Nishant', 13 : 'Shrey', 14
: 'Vicky'}
```

You entered a key which is not available in a dictionary, then it will add that key with respective value.
```
>>>Student [15] = 'Kansal'
>>>Student
{11 : 'Ashi', 12 : 'Nishant', 13 : 'Shrey', 14
: 'Vicky', 15 : 'Kansal'}
```

Deleting Element from a Dictionary

There are following ways to delete elements from a dictionary as follows

(i) Using del Keyword

This keyword is used to delete the key that is present in the dictionary.

Syntax
```
del dictionary_name [key]
```

For example,
```
>>>Teacher = {"Name" : "Ashi", "Subject":
"Math", "Id" : 2546, "Salary": 25000}
>>>Teacher
{'Subject': 'Math', 'Name':
'Ashi', 'Salary' : 25000,
'Id' : 2456}
>>>del Teacher ['Id']
>>>Teacher
{'Subject' : 'Math', 'Name' : 'Ashi', 'Salary'
: 25000}
```

One drawback of this keyword is that if you want to delete key that is not exist in dictionary, then it will give exception error.
```
>>>del Teacher ['Age']
Trackback (most recent call last):
File "<pyshell#4>", line 1, in <module>
    del Teacher ['Age']
KeyError : 'Age'
```

(ii) Using pop () method

This method is used to delete key and respective value from dictionary.

Syntax

```
dictionary_name.pop (key)
```

For example,

```
>>>Teacher = {'Name' : 'Ashi', 'Subject' :
'Math', 'Id' : 2546, 'Salary' : 25000}
>>>Teacher
{'Subject' : 'Math', 'Name' : 'Ashi', 'Salary'
: 25000, 'Id' : 2546}
>>>Teacher.pop ('Id')
2546
>>>Teacher
{'Subject' : 'Math', 'Name' : 'Ashi', 'Salary'
: 25000}
```

Advantage over using del keyword is that it provides the mechanism to print desired value if tried to remove a non existing dictionary pair.

```
>>>Teacher.pop ('Age', "Key not found in
dictionary")
'Key not found in dictionary'
```

Membership Operators

in and not in membership operators are used with dictionary. These operators check whether a specific key is present in dictionary or not. If it is present, then it will give True otherwise False.

Syntax

```
Key in dictionary_name
Key not in dictionary_name
```

For example,

```
>>>Employee = {'Id':4598, 'Name': 'Shubham',
'Dept':'Programmer', 'Salary':35000}
>>>Employee
{'Id':4598, 'Name':'Shubham',
'Dept':'Programmer', 'Salary':35000}
>>>'Age' in Employee
False
>>>'Id' in Employee
True
>>>'Designation' not in Employee
True
```

These operators do not work on values.

```
>>>'Shubham' in Employee
False
```

If you want to used values with in and not in operators then use `dictionary_name.values()` with value's name.

```
>>>'Shubham' in Employee.values()
True
```

Built-in Methods

Python has some built-in methods that dictionary objects can call. Some of them are describe below

(i) len()

This method is used to return the total length of the dictionary.

Syntax

```
len(dictionary_name)
```

For example,

```
>>>dic = {1 : 'This', 2 : 'That', 3 : 'The', 4 :
'World'}
>>>len (dic)
4
>>>del dic[2]
>>>len (dic)
3
>>>dic [5] = 'Hello'
>>>dic [6] = 'Wonder'
>>>len (dic)
5
>>>dic
{1 : 'This', 3 : 'The', 4 : 'World', 5 :
'Hello', 6 : 'Wonder'}
```

(ii) clear()

This method is used to remove the elements of the dictionary. It produces an empty dictionary. It will only delete elements not a dictionary. It does not take any parameter and does not return any value.

Syntax

```
dictionary_name.clear()
```

For example,

```
>>>dic1 = {"Project" : "All In One", "Days" :
15, "Level" : "High"}
>>>dic1.clear()
>>>dic1
{ }
```

If you want to delete the dictionary with its elements, then del keyword is used.

```
>>>dic1 = {"Project" : "All in One", "Days" :
15, "Level" : "High"}
>>>del dic1
>>>dic1
Trackback (most recent call last) :
    File "<pyshell#5>", line1, in <module>
        dic1
NameError : name 'dic1' is not defined
```

(iii) get()

This method returns the value for the given key, if present in the dictionary. It takes maximum of two parameters.

Syntax

```
dictionary_name.get (Key[, value])
```

Here, Key to be searched in the dictionary **value (optional)** value to be returned if the key not found. The default value is None.

For example,

```
>>>Student = {'Name' : 'Shyam', 'Roll No' : 21,
'Marks' : 459, 'Class' : 12}
>>>Student
{'Class' : 12, 'Roll No' : 21, 'Marks' : 459,
'Name' : 'Shyam'}
>>>Student.get ('Name')
'Shyam'
>>>Student.get ('Age', 'Not Found')
'Not Found'
>>>Student.get ('Marks', 'Not Found')
459
```

(iv) items ()

This method returns a view object that displays a list of dictionary's (key, value) tuple pairs. items() method does not take any parameters.

Syntax

```
dictionary_name.items()
```

For example,

```
>>>Teacher = {'Name' : 'Akshat', 'Subject' :
'Science', 'Salary' : 28000, 'Experience' : 4}
>>>Teacher. items ()
dict_items ([('Salary', 28000), ('Subject',
'Science'), ('Experience', 4), ('Name',
'Akshat')])
```

We can also display this using for loop

```
>>>dic = Teacher.items()
>>>for i in dic :
      print (i)
```

Output

('Salary', 28000)

('Subject', 'Science')

('Experience', 4)

('Name', 'Akshat')

(v) keys()

This method returns a view object that displays a list of all the keys in the dictionary. It does not take any parameters.

Syntax

```
dictionary_name.keys()
```

For example,

```
>>>Teacher = {'Name' : 'Akshat', 'Subject' :
'Science', 'Salary' : 28000, 'Experience' : 4}
>>>Teacher.keys()
dict_keys(['Salary', 'Subject',
'Experience', 'Name'])
```

(vi) values ( )

This method returns a view object that displays a list of all the values in the dictionary. It does not take any parameters.

Syntax

```
dictionary_name.values ()
```

For example,

```
>>>Teacher = {'Name' : 'Akshat', 'Subject' :
'Science', 'Salary' : 28000, 'Experience' : 4}
>>>Teacher.values()
dict_values([28000, 'Science', '4',
'Akshat'])
```

(vii) update ( )

This method updates the dictionary with the elements from the another dictionary object or from an iterable of key/value pairs.

Syntax

```
dictionary_name1.update (dictionary_name2)
```

For example,

```
>>>Teacher = {'Name' : 'Akshat', 'Subject' :
'Science', 'Salary' : 28000}
>>>Teacher1 = {'Name' : 'Akansha', 'Salary' :
25000, 'Experience' : 5}
>>>Teacher.update(Teacher1)
>>>Teacher
('Salary' : 25000, 'Subject', 'Science',
'Experience' : 5, 'Name' : Akansha}
```

(viii) sorted ()

This method returns a sorted sequence of the keys in the dictionary.

Syntax

```
sorted (dictionary_name)
```

For example,

```
>>>Teacher = {'Name' : 'Akshat', 'Subject' :
'Science', 'Salary' : 28000, 'Experience' : 4}
>>>sorted(Teacher)
['Experience', 'Name', 'Salary', 'Subject']
```

If a dictionary contains both string and integer as keys, then it will give an error.

```
>>>dic = {'One' : 'This', 2 : 'That', '5' :
'World', 'Five' : 'Wonders'}
>>>sorted (dic)
Trackback (most recent call last):
   File "<pyshell#18>", line 1, in <module>
      sorted(dic)
TypeError : unorderable types : str () < int ()
```

(ix) fromkeys()

This method creates a new dictionary from the given sequence of elements with a value provided by the user.

Syntax
```
dict.fromkeys(seq, value)
```
For example,
```
>>>key = {1, 2, 3, 4, 5}
>>>value = dict.fromkeys (key)
>>>print (value)
{1: None, 2 : None, 3 : None, 4 : None, 5 :
None}
>>>value1 = dict.fromkeys (key, 'Hello')
>>>print (value1)
{1 : 'Hello', 2 : 'Hello', 3 : 'Hello', 4 :
'Hello', 5 : 'Hello'}
```

(x) copy()

This method returns a shallow copy of the dictionary.

Syntax
```
dict.copy( )
```
Here, copy( ) method does not take any parameters.

For example,
```
dic = {1 : 'One', 2 : 'Two', 3 : 'Three'}
dic1 = dic. copy ( )
print ('Original dictionary : ', dic)
print ('Copied dictionary : ', dic1)
```

Output

Original dictionary : {1 : 'One', 2 : 'Two', 3 : 'Three'}

Copied dictionary : {1 : 'One', 2 : 'Two', 3 : 'Three'}

(xi) popitem ()

This method in dictionary helps to achieve similar purpose. It removes the arbitrary key value pair from the dictionary and returns it as a tuple. There is an update for this method from Python version 3.7 onwards.

Syntax
```
dict.popitem( )
```
For example,
```
dic = {'Akshat' : 26, 'Riya' : 24, 'Shrey' :
27}
print ('Before deletion : ', dic)
dic1 = dic.popitem ( )
print ('Deleted element', dic1)
print ('After deletion :', dic)
```

Output

Before deletion : {'Akshat' : 26, 'Riya' : 24, 'Shrey' : 27}

Deleted element : ('Shrey', : 27)

After deletion : {'Akshat' : 26, 'Riya' : 24}

(xii) setdefault ()

This method returns the value of a key (if the key is in dictionary). If not, it inserts key with a value to the dictionary.

Syntax
```
dict.setdefault (key[, default_value])
```
For example,
```
>>>dic = {'Akshat' : 26, 'Riya': 24,
'Shrey':27}
>>>dic1 = dic.setdefault ('Riya')
>>>print ('Dictionary : ', dic)
Dictionary : {'Akshat' : 26, 'Riya' : 24,
'Shrey' : 27}
>>>print ('Founded key : ', dic1)
Founded key : 24
>>> dic1 = dic.setdefault ('Muskan')
>>> print ('Dictionary :', dic)
Dictionary : {'Akshat' : 26, 'Riya' : 24,
'Shrey' : 27, 'Muskan' : None}
>>> print ('Founded key : ' , dic1)
Founded key : None
```

(xiii) max ()

This method is used to return the maximum key from the dictionary.

Syntax
```
max(dict)
```
For example,
```
dic = {'Akshat' : 26, 'Riya' : 24, 'Shrey' :
27}
dic1 = max(dic)
print ('Dictionary : ', dic)
print ('Maximum key : ', dic1)
```

Output

Dictionary : {'Akshat' : 26, 'Riya' : 24, 'Shrey' : 27}

Maximum key : Shrey

(xiv) min ()

This method is used to return the minimum key from the dictionary.

Syntax
```
min(dict)
```
For example,
```
dic = {'Akshat' : 26, 'Riya' : 24, 'Shrey' :
27}
dic1 = min(dic)
print ('Dictionary :', dic)
print ('Minimum key :', dic1)
```

Output

Dictionary : {'Akshat' : 26, 'Riya' : 24, 'Shrey' : 27}

Minimum key : Akshat

Chapter Practice

Objective Questions

• Multiple Choice Questions

1. What will be the output of the following Python code snippet?
```
d1 = {"Neha":86, "Yash":92}
d2 = {"Neha":86, "Yash":88}
d1 > d2
```
(a) True
(b) False
(c) Error
(d) None

Ans. (c) Arithmetic operator '>' cannot be used with dictionaries.

2. What will be the output of the following Python code?
```
Dic1={}
Dic1[2]=85
Dic1[1]=[22,23,24]
print(Dic1[1][1])
```
(a) [22,23,24]
(b) 23
(c) 22
(d) Error

Ans. (b) Now, Dic1={2 : 85, 1 : [22, 23, 24]}. Dic1[1][1] refers to second element having key on position 1, i.e. 23.

3. What will be the output of the following Python code?
```
dic1 = {0: 'One', 1: 'Two', 2: 'Three'}
for x, y in dic1:
    print(x, y)
```
(a) 0 1 2
(b) One Two Three
(c) 0 One 1 Two 2 Three
(d) Error

Ans. (d) It will give Error, because objects of type int are not iterable.

4. What will be the output of the following Python code snippet?
```
d = {"Neha" : 140, "Paras" : 145}
print(list(d.keys()))
```
(a) ["Neha", "Paras"]
(b) ["Neha" : 140, "Paras" : 145]
(c) ("Neha", "Paras")
(d) ("Neha" : 140, "Paras" : 145)

Ans. (a) The output of the code is a list containing only keys of the dictionary d, with the help of d.keys() method.

5. What will be the output of the following Python code snippet?
```
dic1 = { 1 : 'One', 2 : 'Two', 3 : 'Three'}
dic1 = {}
print (len(dic1))
```
(a) 1
(b) 0
(c) 3
(d) 2

Ans. (b) In the second line of code, the dictionary becomes an empty dictionary. Thus, length = 0.

6. What is the output of following code?
```
dic1 ={11, 12, 13}
for i in dic1 :
    print (i)
```
(a) 11 12 13
(b) {11, 12, 13}{11, 12, 13} {11, 12, 13}
(c) Error
(d) None

7. What is the output of following code?
```
>>> dic = {'A' : 'One', 'B' : 'Two' , 'C' : 'Three' }
>>> dic.keys ( )
```
(a) ['B', 'C', 'A']
(b) dict_keys [('B', 'C', 'A')]
(c) dict_keys (['B', 'C', 'A'])
(d) keys (['B', 'C', 'A'])

Ans. (c) keys() returns a view object that displays a list of all the keys in the dictionary.

In given dictionary, A, B, C are keys, while One, Two, Three are values.

8. Which one of the following is correct?
(a) In Python, a dictionary can have two same keys with different values.
(b) In Python, a dictionary can have two same values with different keys.
(c) In Python, a dictionary can have two same keys or same values but cannot have two same key-value pair.
(d) In Python, a dictionary can neither have two same keys nor two same values.

Ans. (b) In Python, a dictionary can have two same values with different keys.

9.
```
d1={"abc":5,"def":6,"ghi":7}
print(d1[0])
```
What will be the output of above Python code?
(a) abc
(b) 5
(c) {"abc":5}
(d) Error

Ans. (d) The given code will show an error. Because 0 is not a key in given dictionary abc, def and ghi considered as keys to the given dictionary.

10. Which of these about a dictionary is false?
(a) The values of a dictionary can be accessed using keys.
(b) The keys of a dictionary can be accessed using values.
(c) Dictionaries are not ordered.
(d) Dictionaries are mutable.

Ans. (b) The values of a dictionary can be accessed using keys but the keys of a dictionary cannot be accessed using values.

11. Keys of a dictionary are
(a) mutable
(b) immutable
(c) Both (a) and (b)
(d) None of these

Ans. (b) Keys of a dictionary must be unique and of immutable data types such as strings, tuples etc. Immutable means they cannot be changed after creation. But in dictionary, key-value can be repeated and be of any type.

12. Dictionaries are also called
(a) mappings
(b) hashes
(c) associative arrays
(d) All of these

Ans. (d) Dictionaries are also called mappings, hashes and associative arrays. These are unordered collection of data values that stored the key : value pair instead of single value as an element. Dictionaries are used to map or associate things you want to store the keys you need to get them.

13. ...... method is used to delete key and respective value from dictionary.
(a) del()
(b) delete()
(c) pop()
(d) remove()

Ans. (c) pop() method removes an element from the dictionary. It removes the element which is associated to the specified key. If specified key is present in the dictionary , it removes and returns its value. If the specified key is not present, it throws an error KeyError.

14. Which function returns the value for the given key, if present in the dictionary?
(a) items()
(b) get()
(c) clear()
(d) keys()

Ans. (b) get() method returns the value for the given key, if present in the dictionary. It takes maximum of two
Syntax `dictionary_name.get (key [,value])`

15. Each key-value pair in a dictionary is separated by
(a) ;
(b) :
(c) ,
(d) <

Ans. (b) Each key-value pair in a dictionary is separated by colon (:) whereas each key is separated by a comma (,).

16. A dictionary is used to .... things you want to store the keys you need to get them.
(a) map
(b) associate
(c) Both (a) and (b)
(d) None of these

Ans. (b) A dictionary is used to map or associate things you want to store the keys you need to get them.

17. Which type of brackets are used to create dictionary?
(a) [ ]
(b) ( )
(c) < >
(d) { }

Ans. (d) Dictionary is listed in curly brackets, inside these curly brackets, keys and values are declared.
Syntax `dictionary_name = {key1 : value1, key2 : value2, ...}`

18. .... operators are used with dictionary to check whether a specific key is present in dictionary or not.
(a) Comparison
(b) Membership
(c) Logical
(d) Access

Ans. (b) in and not in membership operators are used with dictionary to check whether a specific key is present in dictionary or not. If it is present, then it will give True, otherwise False.

19. Which of the following dictionary means putting a dictionary inside another dictionary?
(a) Nested
(b) Sub
(c) Classic
(d) Internal

Ans. (a) Nested dictionary means putting a dictionary inside another dictionary. Nesting is of great use as kind of information we can model in programs expanded greatly.

20. What will be the output of following code?
```
dic = {"Ansh" : 25, "Ritu" : 26}
dic ['Ritu']
```
(a) 25
(b) 26
(c) Ritu : 26
(d) "Ritu" : 26

Ans. (b) In Python, to access the element from a dictionary, keys are used. "Ritu" is the key whose value is 26, so output is 26.

• Case Based MCQs

21. Consider the following dictionary :
```
dic = {1 : [45, 89, 65], 'A' : (23, 45, 6)}
```
Based on the above code, answer the following questions.

(i) Find the output.
```
print (dic.keys())
```
(a) dict_keys (['A', 1])
(b) dict_key ('A', 1)
(c) dict_keys ('A', 1)
(d) dict_key ['A', 1]

(ii) Choose the correct option of given statement.
```
print (dic.values())
```
(a) ([45, 89, 65], (23, 45,6))
(b) dict_values ([45, 89, 65]), (23, 45, 6))
(c) dict_values ([[45, 89, 65], (23, 45, 6)])
(d) dict ([[45, 89, 65],(23, 45, 6)])

(iii) Identify the output of len(dic).
(a) 2
(b) 6
(c) 8
(d) None of these

(iv) Which output is best suited for given statement?
```
dic.get ('A')
```
(a) 23, 45, 6
(b) (23, 45, 6)
(c) [23, 45, 6]
(d) Error

(v) Each key is separated by which symbol?
(a) ; (semicolon)
(b) : (colon)
(c) , (comma)
(d) @ (At the rate)

Ans. (i) (*a*) keys() method returns a view object that displays a list of all the keys in the dictionary. It does not take any parameters.

  (ii) (*c*) values() method returns a view object that displays a list of all the values in the dictionary. It does not take any parameters.

  (iii) (*a*) len() method is used to return the total length of the dictionary. It counts the number of keys present in the dictionary.

  (iv) (*b*) get () method returns the value for the given key, if present in the dictionary. It takes maximum of two parameters.

  (v) (*c*) Each key value pair in a dictionary is separated by a colon (:) whereas each key is separated by a comma (,). In which, key will be a single element and values can be list or list within a list, numbers etc.

PART 2
Subjective Questions

• Short Answer Type Questions

1. How can you add following data in empty dictionary?

Keys	Values
A	Agra
B	Bengluru
C	Chennai
D	Delhi

Ans.
```
dic = {}
dic['A'] = 'Agra'
dic['B'] = 'Bengluru'
dic['C'] = 'Chennai'
dic['D'] = 'Delhi'
```

2. Find the output.
```
Student = {1 : 'Aman', 2 : 'Bablu', 3 :
'Chandan'}
Student [2] = 'Sahil'
print(Student)
Student[4] = 'Aasha'
print (Student)
```

Ans. **Output**

{1 : 'Aman', 2 : 'Sahil', 3 : 'Chandan'}

{1 : 'Aman', 2 : 'Sahil', 3 : 'Chandan', 4 : 'Aasha'}

3. What is the advantage of pop( ) method over a del keyword?

Ans. Advantage of pop( ) method over a del keyword is that it provides the mechanism to print desired value if tried to remove a non-existing dictionary pair.

Syntax
```
dictionary_name.pop(key, 'Text')
```

4. What are in and not in membership operators in dictionary?

Ans. in and not in membership operators are used with dictionary. These operators check whether a specific key is present in dictionary or not. If it is present then it will give True, otherwise False.

Syntax
```
key in dictionary_name
key not in dictionary_name
```

5. Write the short note on

  (i) sorted( )

  (ii) fromkeys( )

Ans. (i) **sorted()** This method returns a sorted sequence of the keys in the dictionary.

  (ii) **fromkeys ()** This method creates a new dictionary from the given sequence of elements with a value provided by the user.

6. Find the output of the following code.
```
my_dict = {'data1' : 200, 'data2' : 154,
'data3':277}
print(sum(my_dict.values()))
```

Ans. **Output**

631

7. Find the output.
```
dic = {'data1' : 200, 'data2' : 56, 'data3': 47}
result = 1
for key in dic:
    result = result*dic[key]
print(result)
```

Ans. **Output**

526400

8. Predict the output.
```
dic = {1 : [45, 89, 65], 'A' : (23, 45, 6)}
print(dic.keys())
print(dic.values())
```

Ans. **Output**

dict_keys(['A', 1])

dict_values ([[45, 89, 65], (23, 45, 6)])

9. Predict the output.
```
dic = {'a' : 1, 'b' : 2, 'c' : 3, 'd' : 4}
print(dic)
if 'a' in dic :
    del dic['a']
print(dic)
```

Ans. **Output**

{'d' : 4, 'a' : 1, 'c' : 3, 'b' : 2}

{'d' : 4, 'c' : 3, 'b' : 2}

10. What is the use of len( ) method in dictionary?

Ans. len( ) method is used to return the total length of the dictionary.

Syntax `len(dictionary_name)`

For example,
```
>>>dic = {1 : 'One', 2 : 'Two',
3 : 'Three', 4 : 'Four'}
>>>len(dic)
4
```

11. Read the code shown below and pick out the keys.
```
d = {"Ansh" : 18, "Varsha" : 20}
```
Ans. "Ansh" and "Varsha"

12. What will be the output?
```
dic = {"Ansh" : 25, "Ritu" : 26}
print (list (dic.keys())
```
Ans. ['Ansh', 'Ritu']

13. Define the popitem ( ) method with its syntax.

Ans. popitem ( ) method in dictionary helps to achieve similar purpose. It removes the arbitrary key value pair from the dictionary and returns it as a tuple. There is an update for this method from Python version 3.7 only.

Syntax `dict.popitem( )`

14. Write the following methods.

(i) max ( )   (ii) min ( )

Ans. (i) **max ()** This method is used to return the maximum key from the dictionary.

Syntax `max(dict)`

(ii) **min ( )** This method is used to return the minimum key from the dictionary.

Syntax `min (dict)`

15. Give an example to iterate over (traversing) a dictionary through all keys value pair?

Ans.
```
dic = {1 : 'One', 2 : 'Two', 3 : 'Three', 4 :'Four'}

print ("Keys : Values")
for i in dic :
        print (i, ":", dic[i])
```

Output

Keys	:	Values
1	:	One
2	:	Two
3	:	Three
4	:	Four

16. Define clear( ) method in dictionary.

Ans. clear( ) method is used to remove the elements of the dictionary. It produces an empty dictionary. It will only delete elements not a dictionary. It does not take any parameter and does not return any value.

Syntax `dictionary_name.clear()`

For example,

```
>>>dic = {1 : 'One', 2 : 'Two'}
>>>dic.clear()
>>>dic
{}
```

17. Write about the setdefault ( ) method with an example.

Ans. setdefault ( ) method returns the value of a key (if the key is in dictionary). If not, it inserts key with a value to the dictionary.

Syntax
```
dict.setdefault (Key [, default_value])
```

For example,
```
dic = {'Anu' : 20, 'Rahul' : 25}
dic1 = dic.setdefault('Anu')
print ('Key : ', dic1)
```
Output
Key : 20

18. When to use tuple or dictionary in Python? Give some examples of programming situations mentioning their usefulness.   **[NCERT]**

Ans. Tuples are used to store the data which is not intended to change during the course of execution of the program.

For example, if the name of months is needed in a program, then the same can be stored in the tuple as generally, the names will either be iterated for a loop or referenced sometimes during the execution of the program.

Dictionary is used to store associative data like student's roll no. and the student's name. Here, the roll no. will act as a key to find the corresponding student's name. The position of the data does not matter as the data can easily be searched by using the corresponding key.

19. Write a Python program to find the highest 2 values in a dictionary.   **[NCERT]**

Ans.
```
dict1={'One':65,'Two':12,'Three':89,'Four':65,'Five':56}
h=0
sh=0
for key in dict1:
    if dict1[key]>h:
        sh=h
        h=dict1[key]
print('highest value',h)
print('second highest value',sh)
```

20. Write a Python program to create a dictionary from a string.

Note: Track the count of the letters from the string.

Sample string : 'w3resource'

Expected output : {'3': 1, 's': 1, 'r': 2, 'u': 1, 'w': 1, 'c': 1, 'e': 2, 'o': 1}   **[NCERT]**

Ans.
```
st = input("Enter a string: ")
dic = {}
for ch in st:
    if ch in dic:
        dic[ch] += 1
    else:
        dic[ch] = 1
for key in dic:
    print(key,':',dic[key])
```

• Long Answer Type Questions

21. Write a Python program to split dictionary keys and values into separate lists.

Ans.
```
dic = {'A' : 'Apple', 'B' : 'Ball', 'C' : 'Cat', 'D' : 'Dog', 'E' : 'Elephant'}
```

```
print("Original Dictionary:",str(dic))
# split dictionary into keys and values
keys = dic.keys()
values = dic.values()

#printing keys and values seperately
print ("keys : ", str(keys))
print ("values : ", str(values))
```
Output

Original Dictionary : {'A' : 'Apple', 'B' : 'Ball', 'C' : 'Cat', 'D' : 'Dog', 'E' : 'Elephant'}

keys : dict_keys (['A', 'B', 'C', 'D', 'E'])

values : dict_values (['Apple', 'Ball', 'Cat', 'Dog', 'Elephant'])

22. Write the short note on following with an example.

(i) update( )

(ii) len( )

Ans. (i) **update( )** This method is used to update the dictionary with the elements from the another dictionary object or from an iterable of key/value pairs.

Syntax
```
dictionary_name1.update (dictionary_name2)
```
e.g.
```
>>>Student = {1:'Ashwani', 2:'Shiva',
3:'Sourabh', 4:'Harsh'}
>>>Student [2] = 'Manish'
>>>Student
```
Output

1 : 'Ashwani', 2 : 'Manish', 3 : 'Sourabh', 4 : 'Harsh'

(ii) **len()** This method is used to return the total length of the dictionary or number of keys.

Syntax
```
len(dictionary_name)
```
e.g.
```
dic = {'A' : 'One', 'B' : 'Two', 'C' :
'Four', 'D' : 'Four'}
dic1 = {'A' : 'One', 'B' : 'Two, 'C' :
'Three', 'D' : 'Four', 'E' : 'Five'}
dic.update(dic1)
print(dic)
a = len(dic)
print('The length is', a)
```
Output

{'A' : 'One', 'B' : 'Two', 'C' : 'Three', 'D' : 'Four', 'E' : 'Five'}

The length is 5

23. Find the output.

(i)
```
x = {(1, 2) : 1, (2, 3) : 2}
print (x[1, 2])
```
(ii)
```
x = {'a' : 1, 'b' : 2, 'c' : 3}
print (x['a', 'b'])
```
(iii)
```
a = {}
a[1] = 1
a['1'] = 2
a[1] + = 1
sum = 0
```
```
for i in a:
    sum = sum + a[i]
print(sum)
```
Ans. (i) 1   (ii) KeyError   (iii) 4

24. Predict the output.

(i)
```
dic = {}
dic[1] = 1
dic['1'] = 2
dic[1.0] = 4
sum = 0
for i in dic:
    sum = sum + dic[i]
print(sum)
```
(ii)
```
dic = {}
dic [(1, 2, 4)] = 8
dic [(4, 2, 1)] = 10
dic [(1, 2)] = 24
sum = 0
for i in dic :
    sum = sum + dic [i]
print (sum)
print (dic)
```
Ans. (i) 6

(ii) 42

{(1, 2) : 24, (4, 2, 1) : 10, (1, 2, 4) : 8}

25. Find the output.

(i)
```
n = {'a' : [2, 3, 1], 'b' : [5, 2, 1], 'c'
: [2, 3, 4]}
sorted_dic = {i : sorted(j) for i, j in
n.items ()}
print(sorted_dic)
```
(ii)
```
dict = {'c' : 789, 'a' : 796, 'b' : 908}
for i in sorted(dict):
    print(dict[i])
```
(iii)
```
students = {'Sahil' : {'Class' : 11,
'roll_no' : 21},
'Puneet' : {'Class' : 11,
'roll_no' : 30}}
for i in students :
    print (i)
    for j in students [i]:
        print (j, ':', students [i][j])
```
Ans. (i) {'b' : [1, 2, 5], 'c' : [2, 3, 4], 'a' : [1, 2, 3]}

(ii) 796

908

789

(iii) Sahil

Class : 11

roll_no : 21

Puneet

Class : 11

roll_no = 30

26. Write a Python program to remove a dictionary from list of dictionaries.

Ans. list1 = [{"id" : 101, "data" : "HappY"},

```
{"id" : 102, "data" : "BirthDaY"},
{"id" : 103, "data" : "Vyom"}]
print("The original list is : ")
for a in list1:
  print(a)
for i in range(len(list1)):
  if list1[i]['id'] == 103:
      del list1[i]
      break
print ("List after deletion of dictionary :")
for b in list1:
  print(b)
```

Output

The original list is :
{'id' : 101, 'data' : 'HappY'}
{'id' : 102, 'data' : 'BirthDaY'}
{'id' : 103, 'data' : 'Vyom'}
List after deletion of dictionary :
{'id' : 101, 'data' : 'HappY'}
{'id' : 102, 'data' : 'BirthDaY'}

27. Find the output of the given Python program.

```
key1 = ["Data 1", "Data 2"]
name = ["Manish", "Nitin"]
marks = [480, 465]
print ("The original key list : " + str(key1))
print ("The original nested name list : " +
str(name))
print ("The original nested marks list : " +
str(marks))
output = {key : {'Name' : name, 'Marks' : marks}
for key, name, marks in zip(key1, name, marks)}
print("The dictionary after creation :",
str(output))
```

Ans. **Output**

The original key list : ['Data 1', 'Data 2']
The original nested name list : ['Manish', 'Nitin']
The original nested marks list : [480, 465]
The dictionary after creation : {'Data 2' : {'Name' : 'Nitin', 'Marks' : 465}, 'Data 1' : {'Name' : 'Manish', 'Marks' : 480}}

28. Write Python program to test if dictionary contains unique keys and values.

Ans.
```
dict1 = {'Manish' : 1, 'Akshat' : 2, 'Akansha' :
3, 'Nikuj' : 1}
print("The original dictionary : " +
str(dict1))
flag = False
val = dict()
for keys in dict1:
  if dict1[keys] in val:
      flag = True
      break
  else :
    val[dict1[keys]] = 1
```

```
print("Does dictionary contain repetition: " +
str(flag))
```

Output

The original dictionary : {'Nikunj' : 1, 'Akshat' : 2, 'Akansha' : 3, 'Manish' : 1}
Does dictionary contain repetition : True

29. Dictionaries are Python's implementation of a data structure that is more generally known as an associative array. A dictionary consists of a collection of key-value pair. Each key-value pair maps the key to its associated value.

You can define a dictionary by enclosing a comma-separated list of key-value pair in curly braces {}. A colon (:) separates each key from its associated value:

(i) What is dictionary?

(ii) Is dictionary mutable or immutable?

(iii) Write the syntax to create dictionary.

(iv) Can we create empty dictionary?

(v) Which feature is used to access the elements from a dictionary?

Ans. (i) Dictionary is an unordered collection of data values that stored the key : value pair instead of single value as an element.

(ii) Dictionary is immutable which means they cannot be changed after creation.

(iii) `dictionary_name = {key1 : value1, key2 : value2, …}`

(iv) Yes, we can create empty dictionary.
For example, `dic1 = { }`

(v) Keys are used to access the elements from a dictionary.

30. Create a dictionary 'ODD' of odd numbers between 1 and 10, where the key is the decimal number and the value is the corresponding number in words. Perform the following operations on this dictionary:

(i) Display the keys

(ii) Display the values

(iii) Display the items

(iv) Length of the dictionary

(v) Check if 7 is present or not

(vi) Check if 2 is present or not

(vii) Retrieve the value corresponding to the key 9

(viii) Delete the item from the dictionary corresponding to the key 9

```
>>> ODD = {1:'One',3:'Three',5:'Five',7:
'Seven',9:'Nine'}
>>> ODD
{1: 'One', 3: 'Three', 5: 'Five', 7: 'Seven',
9: 'Nine'}
```
[NCERT]

Ans. (i) ```>>> ODD.keys()```
```dict_keys([1, 3, 5, 7, 9])```
(ii) ```>>> ODD.values()```
```dict_values(['One', 'Three', 'Five', 'Seven', 'Nine'])```
(iii) ```>>> ODD.items()```
```dict_items([(1, 'One'), (3, 'Three'), (5, 'Five'), (7, 'Seven'), (9, 'Nine')])```
(iv) ```>>> len(ODD)```
```5```
(v) ```>>> 7 in ODD```
```True```
(vi) ```>>> 2 in ODD```
```False```
(vii) ```>>> ODD.get(9)```
```'Nine'```
(viii) ```>>> del ODD[9]```
```>>> ODD```
```{1: 'One', 3: 'Three', 5: 'Five', 7: 'Seven'}```

31. Write a program to enter names of employees and their salaries as input and store them in a dictionary. **[NCERT]**

Ans.
```
num = int(input("Enter the number of employees: "))

count = 1
employee = dict()
while count <= num:
    name = input("Enter the name of the
                            Employee: ")
    salary = int(input("Enter the salary: "))
    employee[name] = salary
    count += 1
    print("\n\nEMPLOYEE_NAME\tSALARY")
for k in employee:
    print(k,'\t\t',employee[k])
```

32. Consider the following dictionary
```
stateCapital = {"AndhraPradesh":"Hyderabad",
"Bihar":"Patna","Maharashtra":"Mumbai",
"Rajasthan":"Jaipur"}
```
Find the output of the following statements.
(i) ```print(stateCapital.get("Bihar"))```
(ii) ```print(stateCapital.keys())```
(iii) ```print(stateCapital.values())```
(iv) ```print(stateCapital.items())```
(v) ```print(len(stateCapital))```
(vi) ```print("Maharashtra" in stateCapital)```
(vii) ```print(stateCapital.get("Assam"))```
(viii) ```del stateCapital["Rajasthan"]```
```print(stateCapital)``` **[NCERT]**

Ans. (i) Patna
(ii) dict_keys(['AndhraPradesh', 'Bihar', 'Maharashtra', 'Rajasthan'])
(iii) dict_values(['Hyderabad', 'Patna', 'Mumbai', 'Jaipur'])
(iv) dict_items([('AndhraPradesh', 'Hyderabad'), ('Bihar', 'Patna'), ('Maharashtra', 'Mumbai'), ('Rajasthan', 'Jaipur')])
(v) 4
(vi) True
(vii) None
(viii) {'AndhraPradesh': 'Hyderabad', 'Bihar': 'Patna', 'Maharashtra': 'Mumbai'}

Chapter Test

Multiple Choice Questions

1. Suppose d = {"Rahul":40, "Riya":45}.

To obtain the number of entries in dictionary which command do we use?

(a) d.size()   (b) len(d)   (c) size(d)   (d) d.len()

2. Which of the following is not true about dictionary keys?

(a) More than one key is not allowed.
(b) Keys must be immutable.
(c) Keys must be integers.
(d) When duplicate keys encountered, the last assignment wins.

3. What will be the output of the following Python code?

```python
a={1:5,2:3,3:4}
a.pop(3)
print(a)
```

(a) {1: 5}
(b) {1: 5, 2: 3}
(c) Error, syntax error for pop() method
(d) {1: 5, 3: 4}

4. What will be the output of the following Python code snippet?

```python
dict1={}
dict1['a']=1
dict1['b']=[2,3,4]
print(dict1)
```

(a) Exception is thrown   (b) {'b': [2], 'a': 1}
(c) {'b': [2], 'a': [3]}   (d) {'b': [2, 3, 4], 'a': 1}

5. What will be the output of the following Python code?

```python
>>> dic1={}
>>> dic1.fromkeys([1,2,3],"Hello")
```

(a) Syntax error   (b) {1:"Hello",2:"Hello",3:"Hello"}
(c) "Hello"   (d) {1:None,2:None,3:None}

Short Answer Type Questions

6. Predict the output.

```python
dic={'a' : 1, 'b' : 2, 'c' : 3, 'd' : 4}
if 'a' in dic :
    del dic['a']
print(dic)
```

7. What is the output of following code?

```python
dic = {}
dic[2] = 1
dic['2'] = 6
dic[2.0] = 8
sum = 0
for i in dic:
    sum = sum + dic[i]
print(sum)
```

8. What is the output of following code?

```python
d = { }
a, b, c, = 1, 2, 3
d[a, b, c] = a + b - c
a, b, c, = 2, 10, 4
d[a, b, c] = a + b - c
print (d)
```

9. What will be the output of the following Python code snippet?

```python
dic1 = {1:'One', 2:'Two', 3:'Three'}
del dic1[1]
dic1[1] = 'Four'
del dic1[2]
print(len(dic1))
```

10. Write any two properties of dictionary keys.

11. Write a program to multiply all the items in a dictionary.

12. Write a Python code to iterate over dictionary using for loop when dictionary is

```python
dic = {'A' : 50, 'B' : 100, 'C' : 150}
```

13. Write a Python code to concatenate following dictionaries to create a new one.

```python
d1 = {'A' : 10, 'B' : 20}
d2 = {'C' : 30, 'D' : 40}
d3 = {'E' : 50, 'F' : 60}
```

Long Answer Type Questions

14. Write Python code which display the nested dictionary.

15. Write Python code to count the frequencies in a list using dictionary.

16. Write Python code to sort the list in a dictionary.

17. Write Python code to convert dictionary to list of tuple.

18. Find the output of the given Python code to swap keys and values in dictionary.

```python
old_dict = {'One' : 742, 'Two':145, 'Three' :
654, 'Four' : 321, 'Five' : 120, 'Six': 365,
'Seven':459, 'Eight': 449}
new_dict = dict([[(value, key)for key, value
in old_dict.items()]])
print("Original dictonary is :")
print (old_dict)
print()
print("Dictionary after swapping is:")
print("Keys:Values")
for i in new_dict:
        print(i, " : ", new_dict[i])
```

Answers

Multiple Choice Questions

1. (b)   2. (c)   3. (b)   4. (d)   5. (b)

Introduction to Python Modules

In this Chapter...

- Importing Modules in a Python Program
- Mathematical Functions
- Random Module/Functions
- Statistics Module

A Python module can be defined as a Python program file which contains a Python code including Python functions, class or variables.

In other words, we can say that our Python code file saved with the extension (.py) is treated as the module. We have a runnable code inside the Python module.

In Python, modules provide us the flexibility to organise the code in a logical way.

Structure of a Python Module

Structure of a Python module consists of different terms, which are as follows

- **doc string** It is useful for documentation purposes and always kept in triple quotes.
- **Variables** It is used for labels of data that are consist in program.
- **Classes** These are essentially a template to create objects.
- **Objects** These are instances of classes. Object is simply a collection of data (variables) and methods (functions).
- **Statements** These are logical instructions which can read and executed by Python interpreter.
- **Functions** It is a self-contained block of statements which are kept together to perform a specific task in related manner.

Importing Modules in a Python Program

To make use of the function in a module, you will need to import the module with an 'import' statement.

Once we import a module, we can directly use all the functions of that module.

Syntax `import module_name`

This gives us access to all the functions in the module(s). To call a function of a module, the function name should be preceded with the name of the module with a dot (.) as a separator.

In Python, import statement can be used in two forms, which are as follows

1. To Import Entire Module

To import entire module, import statement is used. import statement is also used to import selecting modules.

Syntax `import module_name`

When we import a module, we are making it available to us in our current program as a separate namespace. This means that we will have to refer to the function in dot notation, as

```
module_name.function_name
```

e.g.
```
import math
print (math.sqrt (16))
```

Output

4.0

Here, **math** is module which contains the function definition, variables, constants etc., related to mathematical functions.

sqrt () is a function which will find the square root of number that given its in parentheses ().

2. To Import Selected Objects from a Module

When you import modules this way, you can refer to the functions by name rather than through dot notation.

Syntax `from module_name import object_name`

e.g.   `from math import sqrt`
`print (sqrt(16))`

Output

4.0

Here, **math** is module and **sqrt** () is a function. Now, we do not need to use math module with function name, as math.sqrt().

e.g.   `from random import randint`
`for i in range (5):`
`print (randint (1, 20))`

Output

4

10

3

7

9

To Import Multiple Objects

We can also import multiple objects in a single line. To import multiple objects, we can write the multiple objects or functions name using the comma (,) operator.

e.g.   `from math import sqrt, pi`

To Import All Objects of a Module

When you want to import all objects, you can use asterisk (*) symbol at last of keyword import.

Syntax `from module_name import *`

e.g.   `from math import *`

Processing of import <module> Command

When import <module> is issued, following things take place internally

- The code of module which imported is interpreted and executed.
- When module is imported, functions and variables defined in that module are now available to the program.
- To import module, same name as module a new namespace is setup.

e.g. If you imported math module in your program, all objects and attributes of that module would be referred as

     `math.<object_name>`

Processing of from <module> import <object> Command

When from <module> import <object> command is issued, following things take place internally

- The code of module which imported is interpreted and executed.
- When module is imported, only mentioned functions and variables are available to the program.

- In the current namespace, the imported definition is added because no new namespace is setup.

Mathematical Functions

In Python, different number of mathematical operations or functions can be performed by importing the math module which contains the definition of these functions.

Some of the most popular mathematical functions are defined in math module as follows

(i) sqrt ()

This function is used to find the square root of a specified expression or an individual number.

Syntax

`math.sqrt(number)`

For example,
```
>>>import math
>>>s = math.sqrt(4)
>>>print(s)
2.0
>>>s1 = math.sqrt (15)
>>>print(s1)
3.872983346207417
>>>print(math.sqrt (0))
0.0
>>>print(math.sqrt (4.5))
2.1213203435596424
```

If you give negative number as argument it will give an error.
```
>>>s2 = -4
>>>print(math.sqrt(s2))
Trackback (most recent call last):
File "<pyshell#14>", line1,in<module>
    print(math.sqrt (s2))
ValueError math domain error
```

(ii) ceil()

This method returns ceiling value of x i.e. the smallest integer not less than x.

Syntax

`math.ceil(x)`

For example,
```
>>>import math
>>>c = math.ceil(45.23)
>>>print(c)
46
>>>c1 = math.ceil(-76.89)
>>>print(c1)
-76
>>>a = 456.14
>>>print(math.ceil(a))
457
>>>x = math.pi
>>>print(math.ceil(x))
4
```

(iii) floor()

This method is used to return a value which is less than or equal to a specific expression or value.

Syntax

```
math.floor(x)
```

For example,

```
>>>import math
>>>f = math.floor (145.35)
>>>print(f)
145
>>>a = 102.78
>>>print(math.floor(a))
102
>>>b = -75.50
>>>print(math.floor(b))
-75
>>>x = math.pi
>>>print(math.floor(x))
3
```

(iv) pow()

This method offers to compute the power of a number and hence can make task of calculating power of a number easier. In this, two types to calculate power.

- **pow** (x, y) converts its arguments into float and then computes the power.

Syntax

```
pow(x,y)
```

For example,

```
>>>import math
>>>x = 3
>>>y = 4
>>>print(pow(y, x))
64
>>>print(pow(7, 2))
49
>>>print(pow(-3, 2))
9
>>>print(pow(-4, 3))
-64
>>>print(pow(5, -2))
0.04
```

- **pow** (x, y, mod) converts its arguments into float and then computes the power.

Syntax

```
pow(x, y, mod)
```

For example,

```
>>>x = 4
>>>y = 3
>>>z = 10
>>>pow(x, y, z)
4
```

```
>>>pow(5, 3, 7)
6
>>>print(pow(6, 0, 2))
1
>>>pow(0, 4, 2)
0
>>>pow (8, 3, 0)
Trackback (most recent call last):
File "<pyshell#7>", line 1, in <module>
    pow(8, 3, 0)
ValueError : pow() 3rd argument cannot be 0.
```

(v) fabs()

This method returns the absolute value (positive value) of x.

Syntax

```
math.fabs(x)
```

For example,

```
>>>import math
>>>x = -25
>>>math.fabs (x)
25.0
>>>print(math.fabs (65))
65.0
>>>print(math.fabs(-4.3))
4.3
```

(vi) sin()

This method returns the sine of value passed as argument. The value passed in this function should be in radians.

Syntax

```
math.sin(x)
```

For example,

```
>>>import math
>>>x = 65
>>>math.sin(x)
0.8268286794901034
>>>print(math.sin(5.3245521))
-0.8184069203707078
>>>a = math.pi
>>>x = a/4
>>>math.sin(x)
0.7071067811865475
```

(vii) cos()

This method returns the cosine of value passed as argument. The value passed in this function should be in radians.

Syntax

```
math.cos(x)
```

For example,

```
>>>import math
>>>x=9
>>>math.cos(x)
-0.9111302618846769
```

```
>>>math.cos(0)
1.0
>>>print(math.cos(30))
0.15425144988758405
>>>math.cos(-4)
-0.6536436208636119
>>>a = math.pi
>>>math.cos(a)/2
-0.5
```

(viii) tan()

This method returns the tangent of value passed as argument. The value passed in this function should be in radians.

Syntax
```
math.tan(x)
```

For example,
```
>>>import math
>>>x=30
>>>math.tan(x)
-6.405331196646276
>>>math.tan(0)
0.0
>>>math.tan(90)
-1.995200412208242
>>>print(math.tan(-5))
3.380515006246586
```

(ix) pi

It is a mathematical constant, the ratio of circumference of a circle to its diameter.

Syntax
```
math.pi
```

For example,
```
>>>import math
>>>math.pi
3.1415926.....
```

(x) e

It is a mathematical constant.

Syntax
```
math.e
```

For example,
```
>>>import math
>>>math.e
2.71828182846
```

Random Module/Functions

Python offers random module that can generate random numbers. These random modules depend on a pseudo random number that generate function random() and this number generates a random float number between 0.0 and 1.0.

Some random functions are as follows

(i) random()

This method is used to generate a float random number less than 1 and greater than or equal to 0. This function does not require any arguments.

Syntax
```
random.random()
```

For example,
```
>>>import random
>>>random.random()
0.7358047613841759
```

(ii) randint ()

This method is one of methods that handle random numbers. It has two parameters start and end and generate an integer between start and end (including both).

Syntax
```
random.randint(start, end)
```

For example,
```
>>>import random
>>>random.randint(10, 50)
34
>>>print(random.randint(5, 70))
19
>>>random.randint(-80, -20)
-20
>>>random.randint(-12, 60)
35
```

(iii) randrange()

This method returns a random selected element from the range created by the start, stop and step arguments. The value of start is 0 by default. Similarly, the value of step is 1 by default.

Syntax
```
random.randrange(start, stop, step)
```

For example,
```
>>>import random
>>>random.randrange (10, 100, 5)
70
>>>random.randrange(20, 30, 10)
20
>>>random.randrange(-50, -20, 10)
-30
>>>random.randrange(-10, 0, 4)
-6
```

(iv) choice()

This method is used to generate 1 random number from a container. An empty sequence as argument raises an IndexError.

Syntax
```
random.choice (seq/list/tuple/dictionary)
```

For example,
```
>>>import random
>>>random.choice('Programming')
'm'
>>>random.choice([12, 74, 32, 65, 0, 23])
0
>>>random.choice ([12, 74, 32, 65, 0, 23])
65
>>>random.choice ([78, 90, 43, 32, 67])
32
>>>random.choice ({1 : 'One', 2 : 'Two', 3 :
'Three', 4 : 'Four'})
'One'
```

(v) shuffle()

This method randomly reorder the elements in a list. It can shuffle only list elements.

Syntax
```
random.shuffle(list)
```

For example,
```
>>>import random
>>>num = [78, 54, 89, 55, 65, 12]
>>>random.shuffle(num)
>>>num
[78, 89, 12, 54, 65, 55]
>>>random.shuffle(num)
>>>num
[55, 89, 54, 65, 12, 78]
```

Statistics Module

Python is a very popular language when it comes to data analysis and statistics. Python has ability to solve the mathematical expression, statistical data by importing statistics keyword. Statistics module was added in Python 3.4 version. Earlier version of Python cannot access this module. To access Python's statistics functions, we need to import the functions from the statistics module.

Some statistics functions are as follows

(i) mean()

It returns the simple arithmetic mean of data which can be a sequence or iterator. Arithmetic mean is the sum of data divided by the number of data set.

Syntax
```
statistics.mean(data_set)
```

For example,
```
>>>import statistics
>>>list=[45,78,21,32,45,56]
>>>statistics.mean(list)
46.166666666666664
>>>list=[-14,25,-32,-12,0,65]
>>>statistics.mean(list1)
5.333333333333333
>>>t = (14,14,12,32,78)
>>>statistics.mean(t)
30.0
```

```
>>>t1=(-12,-23,45,-2,0,16)
>>>statistics.mean(t1)
4.0
>>>l1=[1.2,2.3,4.5,6,-8]
>>>statistics.mean(l1)
1.2
>>>statistics.mean()
Traceback (most recent call last):
File ''<pyshe||#11>'', line 1, in <module>
    statistics.mean()
TypeError:mean()missing 1 required
positional argument:'data'
```

(ii) median()

This function calculates middle value of the arithmetic data in iterative order. If there are an odd number of values, median() returns the middle value. If there are an even number of values it returns an average of two middle values.

Syntax
```
statistics.median(data_set)
```

For example,
```
>>>import statistics
>>>list=[12,54,89,65,78]
>>>statistics.median(list)
65
>>>list1=[45,-12,-65,78,0]
>>>statistics.median(list1)
0
>>>list2=[-12,4.65,78,-98,45,6.5]
>>>statistics.median(list2)
5.575
>>>t=(78,98,23,-32,8.6,-9)
>>>statistics.median(t)
15.8
```

(iii) mode()

This function returns the number with maximum number of occurrences.

Syntax `statistics.mode(dataset)`

For example,
```
>>>import statistics
>>>list=[45,89,45,78,65,32,45,66]
>>>statistics.mode(list)
45
>>>list1=[4.5,6.5,7.0,6.5,98,4.5,6.5]
>>>statistics.mode(list1)
6.5
>>>t=(-45,-89,0,-89,36,-86,-36)
>>>statistics.mode(t)
-89
```

When two numbers have same occurrence of number then it will give first number of maximum occurrence.
```
>>>list2=[-45,-89,0,-89,36,-36,-36]
>>>statistics.mode(list2)
- 89
```

Chapter Practice

Objective Questions

• Multiple Choice Questions

1. Which module is used for sqrt () to find the square root of a number?

(a) random   (b) square root

(c) math   (d) statistics

Ans. (c) sqrt () is used to find the square root of a specified expression or an individual number. It is performed by importing math module.

Syntax `math.sqrt (number)`

2. Identify the correct output.
```
print (pow(-3, 2))
```
(a) 9   (b) −9

(c) 8   (d) − 8

Ans. (a) pow( ) converts its argument into float and then computes the power. First argument is the number whose power to be find. Here power is 2 which is even number which gives positive result either base number is odd or even.

3. Identify the correct output of
```
>>>import math
>>>f = math.floor (145.35)
>>> print (f)
```
(a) 146   (b) 145

(c) 145.3   (d) 145.4

Ans. (b) floor () is used to return a value which is less than or equal to a specific expression or value.

4. What is returned by math.ceil(7.9)?

(a) 7   (b) 8

(c) 7.0   (d) 9.0

Ans. (b) The ceil function returns the smallest integer that is bigger than or equal to the number itself.

5. To include the use of functions which are present in the random library, we must use the option

(a) import random   (b) random.h

(c) import.random   (d) random.random

Ans. (a) The command import random is used to import the random module, which enables us to use the functions which are present in the random library.

6. What will be the output of the following Python function if the random module has already been imported?
```
random.randint(3.5,7)
```
(a) Error

(b) Any integer between 3.5 and 7, including 7

(c) Any integer between 3.5 and 7, excluding 7

(d) The integer closest to the mean of 3.5 and 7

Ans. (a) The function random.randint() does not accept a decimal value as a parameter. Hence, the function shown above will throw an error.

7. What will be the output of the following Python code?
```
random.randrange(0,91,5)
```
(a) 10   (b) 18

(c) 79   (d) 95

Ans. (a) The function shown above will generate an output which is a multiple of 5 and is between 0 and 91. The only option which satisfies these criteria is 10. Hence, the only possible output of this function is 10.

8. What will be the output of the following Python code?
```
random.randrange(1,100,10)
```
(a) 32   (b) 67

(c) 91   (d) 80

Ans. (c) The output of this function can be any value which is a multiple of 10, plus 1. Hence a value like 11, 21, 31, 41…91 can be the output. Also, the value should necessarily be between 1 and 100. The only option which satisfies this criterion is 91.

9. Which extension is used to save the Python code file?

(a) .Python   (b) .py   (c) .p   (d) .pyth

Ans. (b) Python code file saved with the extension .py is treated as the module. Python module can be defined as Python program file which contains a Python code including Python functions, class or variables.

10. Which of the following symbol is used to import all objects of a module?

(a) *   (b) #   (c) @   (d) $

Ans. (a) When you want to import all objects, you can use asterisk (*) symbol at last of keyword import.

Syntax
```
from module_name import*
```

• Case Based MCQs

11. A Python module is a file containing Python definitions and statements. A module can define functions, classes and variables. A module can also include runnable code. Grouping related code into a module makes the code easier to understand and use. It also makes the code logically organised. When you import a module, the Python interpreter searches for the module in the following sequences.

- The current directory.
- If the module isn't found, Python then searches each directory in the shell variable PYTHONPATH.
- If all else fails Python checks the default path. On UNIX, this default path is normally/usr/local/lib/python/.

(i) To import multiple objects, which symbol is used to write multiple objects?

(a) #
(b) :
(c) ;
(d) ,

(ii) Which of the following module is used in Python?

(a) math
(b) pie
(c) statistics
(d) square root

(iii) Which keyword is used to import the module?

(a) import
(b) import_module
(c) module
(d) Any of the above

(iv) Which of the following module is used for mean(), mode () and median()?

(a) math
(b) arithmetic
(c) statistics
(d) random

(v) Choose the correct syntax to import all objects of a module.

(a) `from module_name import *`
(b) `from module_name import all`
(c) `module_name * from import`
(d) `all module from import`

Ans. (i) (*d*) We can also import multiple objects in a single line. To import multiple objects, we can write the multiple objects or functions name using the comma (,) operator.

(ii) (*a*) math module is used in Python which contains the function definition, variables, constants etc., related to mathematical functions.

(iii) (*a*) To make use of the function in a module, you will need to import the module with an 'import' statement.

Syntax `import module_name`

(iv) (*c*) statistics module is used for mean (), mode () and median (). statistics module was added in Python 3.4 version. Earlier version of Python cannot access this module. To access Python's statistics functions, we need to import the functions from the statistics module.

(v) (*a*) When you want to import all objects, you can use asterisk (*) symbol as last of keyword import.

Syntax `from module_name import*`

• Short Answer Type Questions

1. What will be the output of the given code?
```
import random
random.randrange (1, 50, 10)
```
Ans. The output of this code can be any value which is a multiple of 10, plus 1. Hence, a variable like 11, 21, 31, 41 can be output. Also, the value should necessarily be between 1 and 50.

2. What is return by following code?

(i) `math.ceil(8.7)`

(ii) `math.floor(9.5)`

Ans. (i) 9   (ii) 9

3. What is the output of the given code?
```
from random import shuffle
x = ['One','Two', 'Three', 'Four', 'Five',
                              'Six']
shuffle(x)
print(x)
```
Ans. **Output** ['Four', 'Five', 'Two', 'Six', 'One', 'Three']

4. Write the short note on

(i) ceil()   (ii) floor()

Ans. (i) **ceil()** method returns ceiling value of x i.e, the smallest integer not less than x.

Syntax `math.ceil(x)`

(ii) **floor()** method is used to return a value which is less than or equal to a specific expression or value.

Syntax `math.floor(x)`

5. What is the output of the given code?

(i) `int (math.pow (5, 3))`

(ii) `math.pow(5, 3)`

(iii) `int (pow(5, 3, 4))`

Ans. (i) 125   (ii) 125.0   (iii) 1

6. How can you generate random numbers in Python?

Ans. random module is the standard module that is used to generate a random number. The method is defined as
```
import random
random.random()
```
The statement random.random() returns the floating point number that is in the range of (0, 1). The function generates random float numbers. The methods that are used with the random class are the bound methods of the hidden instances.

7. Define the sqrt() method with an example.

Ans. sqrt() method is used to find the square root of a specified expression or an individual number, math module is used to import this function.

Syntax
```
import math
math.sqrt(number)
```

e.g.
```
>>>import math
>>> math.sqrt(25)
5.0
>>> math.sqrt(16.9)
4.110960958218893
```

8. How to import entire module in Python?

Ans. To import entire module, import statement is used. import statement is also used to import selecting modules.

Syntax `import module_name`

When we import a module, we are making it available to us in our current program as a separate namespace.

9. What things take place internally, when from <module> import <object> command is used?

Ans. • The code of module which imported is interpreted and executed.
  • When module is imported, only mentioned functions and variables are available to the program.
  • In the current namespace, the imported definition is added because no new namespace is setup.

10. Distinguish between floor() and ceil().

Ans. Differences between floor() and ceil() are as follows

floor()	ceil()
It accepts a number with decimal as parameter and returns the integer which is smaller than the number itself.	It accepts a number with decimal as parameter and returns the integer which is greater than the number itself.
Syntax `math.floor()`	**Syntax** `math.ceil ()`

• Long Answer Type Questions

11. Predict the output.
```
import math
print ("cos:", math.cos(1.047197551))
print ("sin:", math.sin(0.523598775))
print ("tan:", math.tan(0.463647609))
print ("degree:", math.degrees(3.1415926))
print ("radian:", math.radians(180))
```

Ans. **Output**

cos : 0.5000000001702586

sin : 0.4999999994818579

tan : 0.49999999999899236

degree : 179.99999692953102

radian : 3.1415926535489793

12. What is the output of the given code?
```
import statistics
from fractions import fraction as F
from decimal import decimal as D
a = statistics.mean ([11, 2, 13, 14, 44])
```

```
b = statistics.mean ([F(8, 10), F(11, 20), F(2,
                                  5), F(28, 5)])
c = statistics.mean ([D("1.5"), D("5.75"),
                      D("10.625"), D("2.375")])
print ("Simple mean:", a)
print ("Fraction mean:", b)
print ("Decimal mean:", c)
```

Ans. **Output**

Simple mean : 16.8

Fraction mean: 147/80

Decimal mean: 5.0625

13. Predict the output.
```
import statistics
list = [5, 2, 5, 6, 1, 2, 6, 7, 2, 6, 3, 5, 5]
x = statistics.mean (list)
print (x)
y = statistics.median (list)
print (y)
z = statistics.mode (list)
print (z)
```

Ans. **Output**

4.230769230769231

5

5

14. Find the output of the following code.
```
import math
print ("ceil:", math.ceil (5.24))
print ("fabs:", math.fabs (5.24))
print ("fabs:", math.fabs (-5.24))
print ("floor:", math.floor (-5.24))
print ("pow:", math.pow (3, 5))
print ("round:", round (3.14159))
print ("round:", round (3.14159,3))
print ("sqrt:", math.sqrt (64))
```

Ans. **Output**

ceil: 6

fabs: 5.24

fabs: 5.24

floor: -6

pow: 243.0

round: 3

round: 3.142

sqrt: 8.0

15. Define the random module in Python.

Ans. Python offers random module that can generate random numbers. There are various types of random functions which can import by random keyword.

Some of them are describe below

  (i) **random()** This method is used to generate a float random number less than 1 and greater than or equal to 0. It does not require any parameters.

  Syntax `random.random()`

(ii) **randint()** This method is one of methods that handles random numbers. It has two parameters start and end generate an integer between start and end (including both).

Syntax `random.randint(start, end)`

(iii) **randrange()** This method returns a random selected element from the range created by the start, stop and step arguments. By default, the value of start is 0 and the value of step is 1.

Syntax `random.randrange(start, stop, step)`

(iv) **choice()** This method is used to generate 1 random number from a container.

Syntax `random.choice(sequence)`

(v) **shuffle()** This method randomly reorder the elements in a list. It can shuffle only list elements.

Syntax `random.shuffle(list)`

16. Modules refer to a file containing Python statements and definitions. A file containing Python code, for example : example.py, is called a module, and its module name would be example. We use modules to break down large programs into small manageable and organised files. Furthermore, modules provide reusability of code. Module focuses on small proportion of the problem, rather than focusing on the entire problem.

(i) The output of the following code is either 1 or 2. State whether this statement is true or false.
```
import random
random.randint (1, 2)
```

(ii) What is module in Python?

(iii) Which function is equivalent to random. randint (4, 7)?

(iv) What is return by math.floor (−20.0)?

(v) How to import modules in Python?

Ans. (i) True

(ii) Modules can define functions that you can reference in other Python files.

(iii) 4 + random. randrange (4) on return any one of 4, 5, 6 and 7.

(iv) 20

(v) Modules can be imported using the import keyword.

17. Write a program to input any two matrices and print sum of matrices. **[NCERT]**

Ans.
```
import random
m1 = int(input ("Enter total number of rows in
the first matrix"))
n1 = int(input ("Enter total number of columns
in the first matrix"))
a = [[random.random() for row in range(m1)] for
col in range (n1)]
for i in range (m1):
    for j in range (n1):
        a[i][j] = int(input())
m2 = int(input ("Enter total number of rows in
the second matrix"))
n2 = int(input ("Enter total number of columns
in the second matrix"))
b = [[random.random () for row in range (m2)]
for col in range (n2)]
for i in range (m2):
    for j in range (n2):
        b [i][j] = int(input ())
c = [[random.random () for row in range (m1)]
for col in range (n1)]
if ((m1 == m2) and (n1 == n2)):
    print("Output is")
    for i in range (m1):
        for j in range (n1):
            c[i][j] = a[i][j] + b[i][j]
    for s in c:
        print(s)
else:
    print("Matrix addition is not possible")
```

18. Write a program to input any two matrices and print product of matrices. **[NCERT]**

Ans.
```
import random
m1 = int(input ("Enter number of rows in first
matrix"))
n1 = int(input ("Enter number of columns in
first matrix"))
a = [[random.random () for row in range (m1)]
for col in range (n1)]
for i in range (m1):
    for j in range (n1):
        a[i][j] = int(input ())
m2 = int(input ("Enter the number of rows in the
second matrix"))
n2 = int(input ("Enter the number of columns in
the second matrix"))
b = [[random.random () for row in range (m2)]
for col in range (n2)]
for i in range (m2):
    for j in range (n2):
        b[i][j] = int(input ())
c = [[random.random () for row in range (m1)]
for col in range (n2)]
if (n1 == m2):
    for i in range (m1):
        for j in range (n2):
            c[i][j] = 0
            for k in range (n1):
                c[i][j] += a[i][j]*b[i][j]
    for s in c:
        print(s)
else:
    print("Multiplication is not possible")
```

Chapter Test

Multiple Choice Questions

1. Which module is used for pow() to find the power of a number?
- (a) random
- (b) math
- (c) statistics
- (d) power

2. Identify the correct output of following code.
```
import math
print (math.floor (153.42))
```
- (a) 153
- (b) 154
- (c) 154.0
- (d) 153.4

3. To include the use of functions which are present in the statistics library, we must use the option
- (a) statistics.h
- (b) import statistics
- (c) import.statistics
- (d) statistics.statistics

4. The value passed in sin() should be in
- (a) degree
- (b) meter
- (c) inch
- (d) radian

5. Which of the following function always gives output in integer form?
- (a) random ()
- (b) choice()
- (c) mean()
- (d) randint()

Short Answer Type Questions

6. What is the output of following code?
```
import math
print(int (math.pow (4, 2)))
print (math.pow (4, 2))
print (math.ceil (4.23))
```

7. What is the output of following code?
```
math.ceil (9.6)
math.floor (9.4)
math.floor (-9.4)
```

8. Identify the output of following code.
```
import math
print ('cos:', math.cos (42.3651))
print ('sin:', math.sin (1))
print ('tan:', math.tan (0))
```

9. Write a short note on
- (i) random()
- (ii) randint()

10. Distinguish between mean() and mode().

Long Answer Type Questions

11. What will be the output of following code?
```
import math
print ('ceil:', math.ceil (8.65))
print ('fabs:', math.fabs (8.65))
print ('fabs:', math.fabs (-8.65))
print ('floor:', math.floor (-8.65))
print ('pow:', math.pow (5, 4))
print ('round:', round (7.654265))
print ('round:', round (7.654265, 2))
print ('sqrt:', math.sqrt (289))
```

12. What is the output of following code?
```
import statistics
list1 = [23, 45, 3, 5, 6, 7, 12, 32, 11, 22,
                                       8, 45]
a = statistics. mean (list1)
print ("Mean is:", a)
b = statistics.median (list1)
print ("Median is:",b)
c = statistics.mode (list1)
print ("Mode is:",c)
```

13. Identify the output of following code.
```
import statistics
from fractions import Fraction as F
from decimal import Decimal as D
a = statistics.mean ([45,65,22,78,65,23,99])
b = statistics.mean ([F(8, 10), F(11, 20), F
(2, 5), F (28, 5)])
c = statistics.mean ([D ('1.5'), D ('5.75'),
D ('10.625'), D('2.375')])
print ('Simple mean:', a)
print ('Fraction mean:', b)
print ('Decimal mean:', c)
```

Answers

Multiple Choice Questions

  1. (b)   *2. (a)*   *3. (b)*   *4. (d)*   *5. (d)*

For Detailed Solutions
Scan the code

Society, Law and Ethics

In this Chapter...

- Issues Related To Cyber Ethics
- Cyber Safety
- Confidentiality of Information
- Cyber Crime
- Computer Security
- Open Source Software
- Software License
- E-Waste Management
- Digital Society and Netizen

The word cyber ethics refers to a code of safe and responsible behaviour for the Internet community. Practicing good cyber ethics involves understanding the risks of harmful and illegal behaviour online and learn how to protect ourselves, and other Internet users from such behaviour.

It is the study of ethics pertaining to computers, encompassing user behaviour and what computers are programmed to, and how this affects individuals and society. Cyber ethics is the moral, legal and social issues relating to cyber technology. It examines the impact that cyber technology has for social, legal and moral systems. It also evaluates the social policies and laws that have been framed in reply to issues generated by the development and use of cyber technology.

Issues Related to Cyber Ethics

There are many advantages of living in an IT world but on contrary, there are many problems which our society is facing today. The crimes like abduction, fraud etc., have increased leaps and bounds. Hence, there are so many ethical issues as far as IT is concerned.

Some of them are as follows:

1. Plagiarism

The word 'plagiarism' has emerged from a latin word plagiarius, which means **kidnapping**. Plagiarism is an act of copying another person's idea, words or work and pretend that they are our own. The intentions behind plagiarism could be malicious or it could be done accidently like copying data from other's computer without his/her

permission and redistributing further. If we talk about the reasons behind plagiarism, then following could be the major factors:

   (i) Fear of failure
   (ii) Not having enough knowledge
   (iii) Being lazy
   (iv) Lack of enforcement
   (v) Competition
   (vi) Lack of management skills

Follow the below given guidelines to avoid plagiarism:

   (i) To avoid plagiarism, instead of copying the language of the book as it is, try to put it in your own language/words.

   (ii) One should have a clear understanding of plagiarism and its consequences, so that no one can perform it unintentionally.

   (iii) If copying someone else's work in our task, word for word, then do not forget enclosing it in quotes and also mention its source.

   (iv) Another way is to credit the author has write which was useful for your task and not taking credit for it yourself.

2. Intellectual Property Rights (IPR)

If someone comes out with a new idea, this original idea is that person's intellectual property.

Intellectual Property (IP) is a legal concept, which refers to creations of the mind for which exclusive rights are recognised. Under intellectual property law, owners are granted certain exclusive rights to a variety of intangible assets such as musical, literary and artistic works, discoveries and inventions, words, phrases, symbols and designs. IPR are the rights given to persons over the creations of their minds. Common types of intellectual property rights include copyright, trademarks, patents, industrial design rights, trade dress and in some jurisdictions trade secrets.

Some of them are as follows:

(i) **Copyright** It includes literary and artistic works such as novels, poems and plays, films, musical works, artistic works such as drawings, painting, photographs and sculptures and architectural designs.

Copyrights are automatically granted to creators and authors. Copyrights law gives the copyright holder a set of rights that they alone can avail legally. It prevents others from copying, using or selling the work. To use other's copyrighted material, one needs to obtain a license from them.

(ii) **Patent** It is usually granted for inventions. Unlike copyright, the inventor needs to apply (file) for patenting the invention. When a patent is granted, the owner gets an exclusive right to prevent others from using, selling, or distributing the protected invention. Patent gives full control to the patentee to decide whether or how the invention can be used by others. Thus, it encourages inventors to share their scientific or technological findings with other. A patent protects an invention for 20 years, after which it can be freely used.

(iii) **Trademark** It includes any visual symbol, word, name, design, slogan, label etc, that distinguish the brand or commercial enterprises.

For example, no company other than Nike can use the Nike brand to sell shoes or clothes. It also prevents others from using a confusingly similar mark, including words or phrases.

Intellectual property rights reserve all the rights of the owner to the information to decide, how much information is to be exchanged shared or distributed.

The protection of intellectual property right of individuals lead to following features.

- It encourages people to create new software as well as helps them to improve the existing applications.
- An environment is provided for the innovative thoughts and technologies.
- Provides the assurity of good returns, people and businesses invest in the national economy.

Violation of IPR

Following are the violation of Intellectual Property Right (IPR):

(i) If a third party were to assume ownership, copy or sell someone's previously copywritten work, that would legally be considered as copyright infringement.

(ii) Copyright law can still be enforced if others try to create simple material from the original source material.

(iii) If a court finds that patent infringement has occurred, the judge will award damages appropriate to compensate for the infringement.

Following are the controls of intellectual property rights:

- Avoid joint ownership
- Get exact match domains
- Safeguard with strong access control

3. Hacking

Hacking means stealing of required information by seeking and exploting weakness in a computer or a computer network.

For gathering required information, a hacker appears with malicious intention and breaks into the owner's system and steals the information illegally.

To prevent hacking, following points are to be used

(i) Create complex passwords.

(ii) Don't give your password to anyone.

(iii) Log out of accounts when you are done with them.

(iv) Make sure you are on an official website when entering password.

4. Piracy

Software piracy means copying of data or computer software without the owner's permission. However, most peoples are aware about piracy and know that it is illegal, yet the piracy is uncontrollable. This is simply the violation of intellectual property rights and right to privacy.

The following are the forms of software piracy:

(i) **Software Counterfeiting** This type of software piracy occurs when fake copies of software are produced in such a way that they appear to be authentic.

(ii) **Softlifting** Purchasing only one licensed copy of a software and distributing and loading it onto multiple systems is called softlifting.

(iii) **Renting** Selling of a software illegally for temporary use as on rent basis is called renting.

(iv) **Hard Disk Loading** Installing an illegal copy of software on the hard disk of a personal computer is called hard disk loading.

(v) **Uploading and Downloading** Creating duplicate copies of the licensed software or uploading and downloading it from the Internet.

In order to stop software piracy, different types of laws as copyright, trademark, patent are used.

Cyber Safety

Cyber safety refers to safety in cyber space. It is a wider concept than the commonly used concept in cyber crime. Cyber safety is the safe and responsible use of Information and Communication Technologies (ICT). Various approaches to cyber safety is founded on

(i) Maintaining a positive approach about the many benefits brought by technologies.

(ii) Encouraging the public to identify the risks associated with ICT.

(iii) Putting in place strategies to minimise and manage risks.

(iv) Recognising the importance of effective teaching and learning programmes.

Safely Browsing the Web

By using a combination of preventative measures and making good choices online you can stay safe when browsing the web. Following are the some precautions for web browsing

Before you Start : Update your Software

Exploiting e-mail and web browsing applications is the most common way hackers and malware try to gain access to devices and your information. Protect yourself before you start browsing the web by make sure that all softwares are up-to-date.

Protect your Web Browser

You can adjust the settings in your web browser to work in a more or less secure way. Most web browsers will give you warnings when they detect you visiting a malicious website. Pay attention to these warnings, they can help to protect you from malware, phishing and identity theft.

Learn more about the Security Settings on your Browser

Settings and security models are different for each browsers, visit the following vendor websites to learn more about the security settings in your browser

(i) Internet Explorer

(ii) Mozilla Firefox

(iii) Google Chrome

(iv) Opera

Identity Theft

It is the act of a person obtaining information illegally about someone else. Thieves try to find information such as full name, middle name, address, date of birth, passwords, phone number, e-mail and credit card numbers. The thief can then use this information to gain access to bank accounts, E-mail, identify themselves as you.

Identity Protection while Using Internet

Your personal identity is important as it defines who you are. Your identity includes your personal information such as name, address, contact information, bank account, credit card numbers and social security numbers should be kept private. We surf the Internet for a variety of reasons from using social media, buying and selling goods etc.. and many more. When we give out our private data to businesses and other internet users such as while filling forms or making payment etc, we trust them to use that information for appropriate purposes.

This is not always the case though and financial and personal data can be used for harmful reasons such as hacking, stalking and identity fraud. Identity fraud is when personal details that have accessed or stolen are used to commit fraudulent acts.

Websites Track You Online in Many Ways

Tracking is generally used by advertising networks to build up detailed profiles for pinpoint ad-targeting even tracking down users for special purpose such as affecting their political choices. The type of information is compiled through your web page usage patterns for tracking you.

This includes the following:

(i) IP Address

The most basic way of identifying you is by your IP address. Your IP address identifies you on the Internet. IP address is a unique address of your device when you connect to Internet. Your computer shares an IP address with the other network devices in your house or office.

From your IP address, a website can determine your rough geographical location. IP addresses can change and are often used by multiple users, so not a good way of tracking a single user over time. An IP address can be combined with other techniques to track your geographical location.

(ii) Cookies and Tracking Scripts

Cookies are small text files that are saved in your web browser when you visit a website. The file might contain your login information, your user preferences, the contents of your online shopping cart and other identifiers. Browser saves the cookies and notes the domain of the website that they belong to. Cookies can also identify you and track your browsing activity across a website.

Cookies can be of the following types:

- **First Party Cookies** By default, first party cookies are allowed in every web browser. First party cookies are user-oriented data packets that are generated and stored locally by the website operator. These are the cookies that store your own login id, passwords for some websites that you frequently visit.

- **Third Party Cookies** Third party cookies are files stored on your computer from advertisers and other parties that have information-sharing agreements with the site you visited. Third party cookies may result in many unwanted advertisements on your web pages.

(iii) HTTP Referrer

When you click the link, your browser loads the web page linked to it and tells the website where you came from.

Fox example, If you clicked a link to an outside website on web page of LIC, the outside website or linked website would see the address of the LIC webpage, you came from. This information is contained in the HTTP referrer header.

The HTTP referrer is also sent when loading content on a web page.

(iv) Super Cookies

A super cookie is a type of browser cookie that is designed to be permanently stored on a user's computer.

It inserted into an HTTP header by an Internet Service Provider (ISP) to collect data about a user's Internet browsing history. Super cookies can be used to collect a wide array of data on user's personal Internet browsing habits including the websites users visit and the time they visit them. These are generally more difficult for users to detect and remove from their devices because they cannot be deleted.

(v) User Agent

The user agent is a browser text string that is given to each website you visit. User agent contains information such as the browser version, compatibility, operating system. Using this data, a website can assess the capabilities of your computer, optimising a page performance and display. Your browser also sends a user agent every time you connect to a website.

Solution to Protect the Identity When Websites Track You Online

All the above things leak your identity information to websites. The most common solution to this is using private browsing or anonymous browsing on Internet.

(i) Private Browsing

This is a privacy feature present in some web browsers that disables web cache, browsing history or any other tracking feature that the browser may have. This allows the user to browse the web without leaving traces such as local data that can later be retrieved.

Private browsing automatically erases your browsing information such as passwords, cookies and history, leaving no trace after you end the session. Private browsing is also known as privacy or incognito mode. There are many other ways to use the Internet without displaying your search history and sharing your data.

- **Incognito Browsing** This is an Internet browser setting that prevents browsing history from being stored. Normally when you visit any web page, text, pictures and cookies required by the page are stored locally on your computer. Incognito mode forgets this data when you close the browser window, or does not store it at all. It is particularly useful if you are entering sensitive data like bank details into the browser, as it can minimise the risk of your information being saved to that computer.

- **Proxy** An Internet proxy is an online computer server that acts as an intermediary between an Internet user and his destination site. Internet users use an Internet Protocol (IP) address to connect to the Internet. This address provides detailed information about the Internet user. When Internet users want to access online information anonymously, they will use an Internet proxy server, which provides a different IP address to the destination website, so that the site does not capture their personal information.

- **Virtual Private Network** (VPN) It is a connection method used to add security and privacy to private and public networks like wi-fi, hotspots and the Internet. A VPN works by using the shared public infrastructure while maintaining privacy through security procedures. However, using a personal VPN is increasingly becoming more popular as more interactions that were previously face-to-face transition to the Internet.

  Privacy is increased with a Virtual Private Network because the user's initial IP address is replaced with one from the Virtual Private Network provider.

Anonymous Browsing

Anonymous browsers allow users to view websites without revealing any personal information like their IP address. One of the most well known anonymous browsers is the Tor browser.

It is an open source piece of software that was originally developed by the united states. It was designed, so that the users could send sensitive information without it being intercepted. Anonymous browsing is popular for two reasons to protect the user's privacy and to bypass blocking applications that would prevent access to websites or parts of sites that the user wants to visit.

Confidentiality of Information

Confidentiality allows authorised users to access sensitive and protected data. Specific mechanisms ensure confidentiality and safeguard data from harmful intruders. Measures undertaken to ensure confidentiality are designed to prevent sensitive information from reaching the wrong people, while making sure that the right or authorise people can infact get it. Access must be restricted to those authorised to view the data. A good example of methods used to ensure confidentiality is an account number or a routing number when online banking. Data encryption is a common method of ensuring confidentiality.

Best practices used to ensure confidentiality are as follows

  (i) Use firewall wherever possible.

  (ii) Control browsers setting to block tracking.

  (iii) Browse privately wherever possible.

  (iv) Be careful while posting on Internet.

  (v) Ensure safe sites while entering crucial information.

  (vi) Carefully handle e-mail.

  (vii) Do not give sensitive information on wireless networks.

  (viii) Avoid using public computers to make sure the following thinks.

  - Browse privately.
  - Do not save your login details.
  - Never save passwords while using public computer.
  - Disable the feature that store passwords.
  - Properly logout before leaving public computer.
  - Clear history and cookies.

Cyber Crime

Cyber crime is defined as a crime in which a computer is the object of the crime (hacking, phishing, spamming) or is used as a tool to commit an offense (child pornography, hate crimes). Cyber criminals may use computer technology to access personal information, business trade secrets or use the Internet for malicious purposes.

Criminals can also use computers for communication and document or data storage. Criminals who perform these illegal activities are often referred to as **hackers**.

Cyber crime may also be referred to as computer crime. Computer systems themselves can be the targets of attack, as when a computer virus is introduced into a system to alter or destroy data.

The most serious computer crimes, however, are committed in the banking and financial-service industries, where money, credit and other financial assets are recorded in electronic databases which are transmitted as signals over telephone lines. e.g. illegally transferring large sums of money to their own accounts. Cyber crime involves the use of computer and network in attacking computers and networks as well.

These are the most common cyber crimes acts as follows

(i) Cyber Bullying

This is the use of technology like the Internet, e-mail, cell phones, social media or picture to harass, threaten, embarrass, or target a person. Cyber bullying is one of the most strong crime committed in the virtual world. On the other hand, global leaders are aware of this crime and pass laws and acts that stop the spreading of cyber bullying. Cyber bullying takes place over cyberspace like physical bullying, cyber bullying is aimed at younger people, such as children and teenagers.

(ii) Cyber Trolls or Cyber Trolling

Trolling has become a more common term for any kind of purposeful online abuse on social media sites like twitter or facebook. Cyber trolls refer to offensive or comments posted online targeting people. Trolling is internet slang for a person who intentionally starts arguments or upsets others by posting inflammatory remarks. The single purpose of trolling is angering people. Trolling is the subset of crime of online abuse, trolls are the new generation of cyber criminals who propagate cyber crime of hate.

(iii) Cyber Stalking

It is a form of cyber crime that takes place online when a criminal uses technology to harass or threaten a person or an organisation. It may include monitoring, identity theft, threats or gathering information that may be used to threaten, embarrass or harass.

Cyber stalking is often including by real time or offline stalking. A stalker may be an online stranger or a person whom the target knows. Cyber stalking is a criminal offense under various state anti-stalking, slander and harassment laws.

(iv) Spreading Rumours Online

Spreading rumours on social media also creates panic and confusion among the public. People should stop from posting wrong information on social media, or comments that could hurt others, the official warned that those who did were risking being punished under the cyber crime law.

Spreading rumours online is a cyber crime and is a punishable offense.

(v) Phishing

It is characterised by attempting to fraudulently acquire sensitive information such as passwords, credit cards details etc., by masquerading as a trustworthy person. Victims receive a malicious e-mail or a text messages that imitates a person or an organisation they trust like a bank or a government office.

When the victim opens the e-mail or text, they find a scary message meant to overcome their better judgement by filling them with fear. The message demands that the victim go to a website and take immediate action or risk some sort of consequence.

If users click the link, they are sent to an imitation of a legimate website. From here they are asked to log in with their username and password credentials. If they are innocent enough to comply, the sign on information goes to the attacker, who uses it to steal identities, thieve bank accounts and sell personal information on the black market.

(vi) Ransomware

This is another kind of cyber crime where the attacker gains access to the computer and blocks the user from accessing, usually by encrypting the data. The attacker blackmails the victim to pay for getting access to the data or sometimes threaten to publish personal and sensitive information or photographs unless a ransom is paid.

Ransomware can get downloaded when the users visit any malicious or unsecure websites or download software from doubtful repositories. Some ransomware are sent as email attachments in spam mails. It can also reach our system when we click on a malicious advertisement on the Internet.

Factors in Rise of Cybercrimes

- **Spread of Computers** Computers are becoming more accessible as their cost decreases, leading to a marked growth in their use, particularly in personal and mobile computing. Many home and even business users are unaware of the potential threats from computer crime or may not possess the technical skills to ensure their own security. This greatly increases the risks of cybercrime.

- **Increasing Use of Broadband** These connections allow greater volumes of network traffic, and when coupled with poorly implemented security measures, increase the likelihood of computer attack.

- **Increasing Financial Motivation for Computer Crime** Information security expert, suggest that the motives behind computer crime have changed. Traditionally, it was motivated by desire for peer recognition and to demonstrate technical skills. However, it is now increasingly financially motivated. The growth of E-commerce with 45% of Internet users participating in some form and the dependence of many aspects of financial life on computers have motivated this shift.

Preventing Cyber Crime

Following points can be considered as safety measures to reduce the risk of cyber crime:

(i) Take a regular backup of important data.

(ii) Use an antivirus software and keep it updated always.

(iii) Do not visit or download anything from untrusted websites.

(iv) Use strong password for web logic and change it periodically. Ignore common words or names in password.

(v) While using someone else's computer, do not allow browser to save password or auto fill data and try to browse in your private browser window.

(vi) Always secure wireless network at home with strong password and regularly change it.

(vii) Always update the system software which includes the Internet browser and other application software.

Computer Security

Computer security is also known as **cyber security** or **IT security**. Computer security is a branch of information technology known as **information security**, which is intended to protect computers. It is the protection of computing systems and the data that they store or access. Most computer security measures involve data encryption and passwords.

Data encryption is the translation of data into a form that is unintelligible without a decode mechanism. A password is secret word or phrase that gives a user access to a particular program or system.

Malware : Threats to Computer Security

Computer systems are vulnerable to many threat that can inflict various types of damage resulting in significant losses.

A threat is a potential violation of security and when threat gets executed, it becomes an attack. Those who execute such threats are known as **attackers**.

Malware stands for **malicious software**. It is a broad term that refers to a variety of malicious programs that are used to damage computer system, gather sensitive information, or gain access to private computer systems. Malware is an unwanted software that any unauthorized person wants to run on your computer.

These are also known as **security threats.** It includes computer viruses, worms, trojan horses, rootkits, spyware, adware etc.

Some of them are described below

(i) VIRUS

VIRUS stands for Vital Information Resources Under Seige.

Computer viruses are small programs that can negatively affect your computer. It obtains control of a PC and directs it to perform unusual and often destructive actions.

Virus copy itself and attaches itself to other programs which further spread the infection. The virus can affect or attack any part of the computer software such as the boot block, operating system, system areas, files and application program. On the other hand, it is also true that not all computer problems are caused by computer viruses. This could be caused by other things such as an error (bug) or a misconfiguration of software or hardware.

For example, Bomber, Whale, OneHaff, KoKo, Eliza etc.

Some common types of viruses are as follows

- Resident Virus
- Direct Action Virus
- Overwrite Virus
- Boot Sector Virus
- Macro Virus
- File System Virus
- Polymorphic Virus
- FAT Virus
- Multipartite Virus
- Web Scripting Virus

Effects of Virus

There are many different effects that viruses can have on your computer, depending on the types of virus.

Some viruses can

- monitor what you are doing.
- slow down your computer's performance.
- destroy all data on your local disk.
- affect on computer networks and the connection to Internet.
- increase or decrease memory size.
- display different types of error messages.
- decrease partition size.
- alter PC settings.
- display arrays of annoying advertising.
- extend boot times.
- create more than one partitions.

(ii) Worms

A computer worm is a standalone malware computer program that replicates itself in order to spread to other computers. Often, it uses a computer network to spread itself, relying on security failures on the target computer to access it. Unlike a computer virus, it does not need to attach itself to an existing program. Worms almost always cause atleast some harm to the network, even if only by consuming bandwidth, whereas viruses almost always corrupt or modify files on a targeted computer. Worms are hard to detect because they are invisible files.

For example, Bagle, I love you, Morris, Nimda etc.

(iii) Trojan

A Trojan or **Trojan Horse** is a non-self-replicating type of malware which appears to perform a desirable function but instead facilitates unauthorized access to the user's computer system. Trojans do not attempt to inject themselves into other files like a computer virus. Trojan horses may steal information, or harm their host computer systems. Trojans may use drive-by downloads or install via online games or Internet-driven applications in order to reach target computers. Unlike viruses, Trojan horses do not replicate themselves.

For example, Beast, Sub7.Zeus, ZeroAccess Rootkit etc.

(iv) Spyware

It is a program which is installed on a computer system to spy on the system owner's activity and collects all the information which is misused afterwards. It tracks the user's behaviour and reports back to a central source. These are used for either legal or illegal purpose. Spyware can transmit personal information to another person's computer over the Internet.

Spyware can harm you in many ways such as

- Malware will log your keystrokes.
- Steal your passwords.
- Observe your browsing choices.
- Spawn pop-up windows.
- Send your targeted e-mail.
- Redirect your web browser to phishing pages.
- Report your personal information to distant servers.
- Can alter your computer settings (like web browser home page settings or the placement of your desktop icons).
- Can affect the performance of your computer system.

  For example, CoolWeb Search, FinFisher, Zango, Zlob Trojan, Keyloggers etc.

Symptoms of a Malware Attack

There are list of symptoms of malware attack which indicate that your system is infected with a computer malware.

Some primary symptoms are as follows

- Odd messages displaying on the screen.
- Some files are missing.
- System runs slower.
- PC crashes and restart again and again.
- Drives are not accessible.
- Anti-virus software will not run or installed.
- Unexpected sound or music plays.
- The mouse pointer changes its graphic.
- Receive strange e-mails containing odd attachments or viruses.

- PC starts performing functions like opening or closing windows, running programs on its own.

Solutions to Computer Security Threats

To safe the computer system from unauthorized access and threats, it is necessary to design some safeguards that handles these threats efficiently.

Some safeguards (or solutions) to protect a computer system from accidental access, are described below

(i) Antivirus (Virus Cleaner)

It is an utility program or set of programs that are designed to prevent, search, detect and remove viruses and other malicious programs like worms, trojans, adware and many more. It is very important to use an antivirus software for users, who use Internet because a computer without antivirus may get infected within few minutes. e.g. Symantec, Norton, Avg, McAfee, Quick Heal etc.

(ii) Digital Certificate

It is the attachment to an electronic message used for security purposes. The common use of a digital certificate is to verify that a user sending a message is who he or she claims to be, and to provide the receiver with the means to encode a reply. It provides a means of proving your identity in electronic transactions. The digital certificate contains information about whom the certificate was issued to, as well as the **certifying authority** that issued it.

(iii) Digital Signature

A digital signature authenticates electronic documents in a similar manner a handwritten signature authenticates printed documents. It is an electronic form of a signature that can be used to authenticate the identity of the sender of a message or the signer of a document, and also ensure that the original content of the message or document that has been sent is unchanged. Digital signatures are easily transportable and cannot be imitated by someone else. Also, the signer of a document cannot later disown it by claiming that the signature was fake.

(iv) Firewall

A firewall can either be software-based or hardware-based and is used to help keep a network secure.

Its primary objective is to control the incoming and outgoing network traffic by analyzing the data packets and determining whether it should be allowed through or not, based on a predetermined rule set.

A network's firewall builds a bridge between an internal network that is assumed to be secure and trusted, and another network, usually an external (inter) network, such as the Internet, that is not assumed to be secure and trusted.

There are two forms of firewall

- **Hardware (External) Firewall** It provides protection to a local network. It is physical device that sits between the computer and the Internet. Hardware firewall requires quite a bit of work to fully configure.

These may range from a simple router to a proxy server that directs all traffic to a server elsewhere on the Internet before sending or taking data from a computer or a network.

- **Software (Internal) Firewall** It installed directly into the computer as programs. Once installed, these firewalls activate themselves and set up with relative ease.

(v) Password

A password is a secret word or a string of characters used for user authentication to prove identity or access approval to gain access to a resource, which should be kept secret from those who are not allowed to get access.

In modern times, user names and passwords are commonly used by people during a log in process that controls access to protected computer operating systems, mobile phones, ATMs etc.

A password is typically somewhere between 4 to 16 characters, depending on how the computer system is set up.

When a password is entered, the computer system is careful not to display the characters on the display screen, in case others might see it.

There are two common modes of password as follows

- **Weak Password** Easily remember just like names, birth dates, phone number etc.
- **Strong Password** Difficult to break and a combination of alphabets and symbols.

Some Other Threats to Computer Security

Adware These are the kind of unwanted programs which appear on your computer as advertisement. They harm the network bandwidth, slow down the speed of your computer, change the home page of your computer and reduce the stability and usability of your system.

Eavesdropping In computer security, this is defined as the unauthorised interception of a conversation, communication or digital transmission in real time. The various forms of communication include phone calls, E-mails, instant messages or any other Internet service.

Spam It is the abuse of messaging systems to send unsolicited bulk messages in the form of E-mails. It is a subset of electronic spam involving nearly identical messages sent to numerous recipients by E-mails.

Open Source Software

Open source refers to something that can be modified and shared as its designed publicly accessible.

Open Source Software (OSS) is any computer software that is distributed with its source code available for modification.

Examples of Open Source Software are Linux, Unix, MySQL etc.

To be considered as open source software by the software development industry, certain criteria must be met as follows

(i) Software must be available free or at a low cost.

(ii) Source code must be included.

(iii) Anyone must be allowed to modify the source code.

(iv) Modified versions can be redistributed.

Criteria for the Distribution of OSS

Open source software is normally distributed with the source code under an open source license.

The distribution terms of open source software must comply with the following criteria :

(i) **Free Redistribution** The license shall not restrict any party from selling or giving away the software distribution containing programs from several different sources. The license shall not require a royalty or other fee for such sale.

(ii) **Source Code** The program must include source code and allows distribution with source code as well as a compiled form. The source code must be in the preferred form in which a programmer would modify the program.

(iii) **Integrity of The Author's Source Code** The license may restrict source code from being distributed in modified form only if the license allows the distribution of "patch files" with the source code for the purpose of modifying the program at build time.

Software License

A software license is a license agreement that gives an individual, a company or an organisation permission to use a software program. It typically provides end users with the right to one or more copies of the software without violating copyrights. The license also defines the responsibilities of the parties entering into the license agreement and may impose restrictions on how the software can be used.

Types of Software License

Software licenses typically are the either proprietary or free and open source. The distinguishing feature being the terms under which users may redistribute or copy the software for future development or use.

(i) Proprietary Software License

The hallmark of proprietary software license is that the software publisher grants the use of one or more copies of software under the End-User License Agreement (EULA), but ownership of those copies remains with the software publisher. This feature of proprietary software licenses means that certain rights regarding the software are reserved by the software publisher.

In other words, without acceptance of the license, the end user may not use the software at all. One example of such a proprietary software license is the license for Microsoft Windows.

Sometimes one can choose between perpetual (permanent) and annual license. For perpetual licenses, one year of maintenance is often required, but maintenance renewals are discounted. For annual licenses, there is no renewal, a new license must be purchased after expiration.

(ii) Free and Open Source Software License

It refers to the software that users can safely run, adopt and redistribute without legal restraint. Open source software refers to freedom to use, share and/or modify the source code and allow copies to other users. Open source softwares are further classified into Permissive license and Copyleft license.

- **Permissive License** Those with the aim to have minimal requirements about how the software can be redistributed are called permissive license. It permits using copying, modifying, merging, publishing, selling and distribution without the source code. Examples of permissive license are as follows:

  (a) **MIT License** It is a permissive free software license originating at the Massachusetts Institute of Technology (MIT) in the late 1980s.

  It is compatible because it can be re-licensed under other licenses. MIT license basically allows developers to modify source code according to their preferences. The MIT license also permits reuse within proprietary software, provided that either all copies of the licensed software include a copy of the MIT license terms and the copyright notice.

  (b) **BSD License** It represents a family of permissive free software licenses that have fewer restrictions on distribution compared to other free software licenses. There are two important versions of BSD license.

  (c) **Modified BSD License or 3-clause License** It allows unlimited redistribution for any purpose as long as its copyright notices and the license's disclaimers of warranty are maintained.

  The license also contains a clause restricting use of the names of contributors for support of a derived work without specific permission.

  (d) **Simplified BSD License or 2-clause License** The simplified BSD license is different from new BSD license (3-clause) license in the sense that it omits the non-endorsement clause.

  (e) **Apache License** It is a permissive free software license written by the Apache Software Foundation (ASF). It allows users to use the software for any purpose to distribute it, to modify it and to distribute modified versions of the software under the terms of the license. Through open source code, apache encourages users to voluntarily improve the design of the software.

- **Copyleft License** Copyleft is a method for making a software program free, while requiring that all modified and extended versions of the program also be free and released under the same terms and conditions. When an open source software project is published with a copyleft license, other developers have the right to use, modify and share the work as long as the reciprocity obligation is maintained.

Examples of copyleft license are as follows:

  (a) **GNU GPL (General Public License)** GPL is a copyleft license. This means that any software is written based on any GPL component must be released as an open source. The result is any software that uses any GPL open source component is required to release its full source code and all of the rights to modify and distribute the entire code. The GPL is based on four freedom to use the source code for any purpose, the freedom to make modification, the freedom to share the source code with anyone and the freedom to share changes.

  (b) **CC (Creative Common) License** CC is an internationally active non-profit organisation that provides free licenses for creators to use when making their source code available to the public. These licenses help the creator to give permission for others to use the source code in advance under certain conditions.

  Every CC license allows you to :

  - Copy the source code (e.g. download, upload etc.)
  - Distribute the source code (e.g. provide copies of the code)
  - Communicate the source code (e.g. make the code available online)

  (c) **GNU Lesser General Public License (LGPL)** It is a free software license published by the Free Software Foundation (FSF).

  The license allows developers and companies to use and integrate a software component released under the LGPL into their own software without being required by the terms of a strong copyleft license to release the source code of their own components. One feature of LGPL is the permission to relicense under the GPL any piece of software which is received under the LGPL. This feature allows for direct reuse of LGPLed code in GPLed libraries and applications.

Open Data

The data that is freely available to everyone to use and republish according to their own requirement, without any restrictions is called open data.

Open data includes non-textual material such as mathematical and scientific formulae, bioscience, biodiversity etc.

Privacy

The right to privacy refers to the concept that one's personal information to be protected from public scruting. Privacy is related to the personal information and, the major issues regarding an individual's right to privacy in the context of computing information related to the following main information functions :

   (i) Collecting information

   (ii) Storing information

   (iii) Distributing information

The right to privacy also involves decisions related to queries like-what information about an individual or other person must revealed to others, under what conditions and with what safety measures? Hence, the risk of invading other's privacy is becoming more serious, as the role of information technology in decision making is increasing day-by-day. With the increase the use of Internet as the means of information transmission, Internet can affect the privacy rights of a person. A person's Internet usage and transaction done by him/her generates a large amount of information, which provides insights into that person's interests and other vital information.

But, in order to preserve personal information, it is suggested not to use computers to gather, save or distribute information that exclusively belongs to some other person.

How to Safeguard User Privacy?

To ensure that the user privacy is not compromised, following measures must be taken:

   (i) The merchant or the seller must clearly state about how the user data will be used, in the terms and conditions of its site application.

   (ii) The merchant or seller must ensure that the user has gone through the terms and conditions given on its site application prior for making any transactions.

   (iii) The merchant must assure the user about data safety by implementing proper safety and security measures such as https protocol and other security mechanism so that users' data is safe from hackers too.

   (iv) The user must go through the terms and conditions of the seller/merchant site before providing any sensitive information and make sure that the site is a safe by checking https protocol and padlock sign etc.

Privacy Laws

Privacy laws refer to the laws that deal with the regulation, storing and using of personally identifiable information, personal healthcare information and financial information of individuals, which can be collected by governments, public or private organisations or other individuals. Privacy laws are considered within the context of an individual's privacy rights or within reasonable expectation of privacy.

Information Technology Act, 2000 has two sections relating to privacy as

   (i) **Section 43A** It deals with implementation of reasonable security practices for sensitive personal data or information and provides for compensation to a person affected by wrongful loss or wrongful gain.

   (ii) **Section 72A** It provides for imprisonment for a period of upto 3 years or/and a fine of upto ₹ 5,00,000 to a person who causes wrongful loss or wrongful gain by disclosing personal information about another person while providing services under the terms of lawful contract.

IT (Information Technology)

Information technology is application of computers and telecommunication equipment store, retrieve, transmit and manipulate data. IT is generally not used in reference to personal or home computing and networking. IT refers to anything related to computing technology, such as networking, hardware, software, Internet or the people that work with these technologies.

Importance of Information Technology in various Fields

Each field has been changed using information technology below:

(i) In Business

Using IT, businesses have the ability to view changes in the global markets far faster than they usually do. They purchase software package and hardware that helps them get their job done. Information technology has allowed businesses to keep up with the supply and demand as consumes grow more anxious to have their items instantly.

(ii) In Education

With so much focus placed on education, it can sometimes be difficult to hold a job and still get the training needed to get a better job. IT plays a key role in students being able to keep their jobs and go to school. Information technology is helping to prevent more high school and college dropouts as well.

(iii) In Finance

IT might just working its hardest with Internet transactions. As more transactions are done, the Internet requires more networks, more computers and more security programs to keep its consumers safe. Information technology has also made it faster and easier than ever to send or receive money. This allows lenders, insurance companies and businesses to run a quick credit check on you making it far easier to open credit.

(iv) In Healthcare

Improvements in information technology have allowed for great reform in healthcare. You can read about the privacy of your online medical records from HHS. Learn about changes in the healthcare industry with an online class.

(v) In Security

With so many transactions done online and so much information available online, it is important to keep all of that safe. IT makes it possible for your online data to stay secure until accessed by the proper channels. Information technology hides your personal digital data away and the only way it can be accessed is by companies who have permission from you.

Introduction to IT Act 2000

The Information Technology Act, 2000 (also known as IT Act or IT A-2000) is an Act of the Indian Parliament notified on 17 October 2000. An Act to provide legal recognition for transactions carried out by means of electronic data interchange and other means of electronic communication. Commonly referred to as "electronic commerce", which involves the use of alternatives to paper-based method, of communication and storage of information, to facilitate electronic filing of documents with the government agencies.

The origin at Act contained 94 sections, divided in 19 chapters and 4 schedules. The laws apply to the whole of India. Persons of other nationalities can also be indicted under the law, if the crime involves a computer or network located in India.

The formations of controller of Certifying Authorities was directed by the Act, to regulation issuing of digital signatures. It also defined cyber crimes and prescribed penalties for them. It also established a cyber Appellate Tribunal to resolve disputes rising from this new law.

Amendments

A major amendment was made in 2008. It introduced the section 66A which penalised sending of "offensive message". It also introduced the section 69, which gave authorities the power of interception or monitoring or decryption of any information through any computer resource. It also introduced penalties for child porn, cyber terrorism and voyeurism. It was passed on 22 December 2008 without any debate in Lok Sabha. The next day it was passed by Rajya Sabha. It was signed by the President of 5 February 2009.

Objectives of IT Act

(i) To stop computer crime and protect privacy of Internet users.

(ii) To make more power to IPO, RBI and Indian evidence Act for restricting electronic crime.

(iii) To give legal recognition for keeping books of accounts by bankers and other companies in electronic form.

(iv) To give legal recognition to digital signature for accepting any agreement *via* computer.

(v) To provide facility of filling document online relating to school admission or registration in employment exchange.

(vi) To give legal recognition to any transaction which is done by electronic way or use of Internet.

Scope of IT Act

(i) IT Act 2000 is not applicable on the attestation for making will of any body. Physical attestation by two witnesses is must.

(ii) Attestation for giving power of attorney of property is not possible *via* electronic record.

(iii) A contract of sale of any immovable property.

(iv) IT Act 2000 is not applicable on the attestation for creating trust *via* electronic way. Physical attestation is must.

Features of IT Act 2000

(i) It helps to promote E-commerce.

(ii) It includes high penalty for cyber crime.

(iii) It provides filing online forms.

(iv) It enhances the corporate business.

Technology and Society

ICT (Information and Communication Technology) are general purpose technologies whose value and impact arise primarily from their use in other economic and social sectors. Three capabilities are especially important for economic and social development as

(i) Enable greater efficiency in economic and social processes.

(ii) Enhance the effectiveness of co-operation between stake holders.

(iii) Increase the volume and range of information available to people, businesses and governments.

Societal Issues by Technology

(i) **Lack of social skills** Frequency of interacting personally has been reduced much thus kids and teenagers are deprived of basic social manner.

(ii) **Poor sleeping habit** Endorsing online activities have affected the sleeping pattern of people.

(iii) **Addiction** Addiction of technology is not less than the drug addiction.

(iv) **Depression** Dependence on technology and less interaction with fellow human beings can lead to depression.

(v) **Lack of privacy** People are opening up their private space by giving their information on social sites giving rise to criminal activities.

Cultural Changes Induced by Technology

(i) **Online shopping** Use of online shopping has changed the culture of going out to the market and buying goods.

(ii) **Home delivery of foods** Online home delivery of foods have changed the culture of going out for a dinner or lunch with family and also the culture of home cooked food.

(iii) **Social media** Social media has changed the culture of going to a friends place to have a chitchat.

E-Waste Management

E-Waste (Electronic Waste) comprises of the electronic products that are no longer useful to us. Electronic Waste may also be defined as discarded computers, office electronic equipment, entertainment electronics device, mobile phones, television sets and refrigerators. It includes used electronics which are destined for reuse, resale, salvage, recycling or disposal. E-Waste management has become a significant problem due to the technical process, we have gained in the last century.

E-Waste Disposal Process

E-Waste is categorized by the government of India under the broad class of hazardous waste. Within E-Waste, there are several categories such as large and small household appliances, electrical and electronic toys and sporting tools, computer and related equipment.

Composition of E-Waste

E-Waste is mostly made up of metal and plastic components, but also contain small amounts of heavy metals and substances of concern (e.g. in printed circuit boards). The wide variety of E-Waste makes it hard to generalise the material content.

For example, Fridges and air conditioners in particular contain refrigerants to enable cooling to take place, but these refrigerants may also contribute to ozone layer depletion or climate change. The E-Waste management involves proper recycling and recovery of the disposed material. The recycle and recovery includes the following unit operations:

(i) Dismantling

E-Waste dismantling process at techlogic process is a mix of reuse and recycling of electronic waste through a mix of manual and automated process, bringing about zero environmental impact and maximizing value from the process of E-Waste disposal.

Removing of parts containing dangerous substances (e.g. Switches), removal of easily accessible parts containing valuable substances (cable containing copper, steel, iron, metal containing parts).

(ii) Segregation of Ferrous Metal, Non-ferrous Metal and Plastic

Scrap metal both ferrous and non-ferrous present in industrial wastes, slags, smelter biproducts, sludges, refinery sweepings etc. can be reclaimed in most instances at a profit and thus are made available for reuse in industry. Very substantial stockpiles of these scrap metal wastes are available for processing in the various industrial areas. This separation is done in a shredder process.

(iii) Refurbishment and Reuse

Refurbishment and reuse of E-Waste has potential for those used electrical and electronic equipment which can be easily refurbished to put to its original use.

(iv) Recycling/Recovery of Valuable Materials

Ferrous metals in electrical are furnaces, non-ferrous metals in smelting plants, precious metals in separating works.

(v) Treatment/Disposal of Dangerous Materials and Waste

Shredder light fraction is disposed of in landfill sites or sometimes incinerated, chlorofluorocarbons (CFCs) are treated thermally, Printed Circuit Board (PCB) is incinerated or disposed of in underground storages, Mercury (Hg) is often recycled or disposed of in underground landfill sites.

Advantages of E-Waste Recycling

If you have electronic items which have stopped working and as good as waste matters, it is a good idea to opt for E-Waste recycling. The key advantages are:

(i) Conserves Natural Resources

Recycling recovers valuable materials from old electronics that can be used to make new products. As a result, we save energy, reduce pollution, reduce greenhouse gas emissions and save natural resources by extracting fewer raw materials from the Earth.

(ii) Protects Environment

E-Waste recycling provides proper handling and management of toxic chemical substances like mercury, lead and cadmium contained in the E-Waste stream.

(iii) Create Jobs

E-Waste recycling creates new jobs for professional recyclers and creates a second market for the recycled materials.

(iv) Saves Landfill Space

E-Waste is a growing waste stream. Recycling these items will help conserve landfill space.

(v) Save Money

Electronics, old water bottles and other trash can be sold for cash.

So if you sell them, you not only save the environment, but make money as well. If you buy recycled materials, which costs less than the new ones, you will also save money.

Disadvantages of E-Waste Recycling

Some disadvantages of E-Waste recycling are as follows :

(i) More Pollution and Energy Consumption

It's contradicting, but the reality is that recycling tons of garbage will require waste to be transported, sorted, cleaned and processed in separate factories, all of which need energy and may result in by-products that can pollute air, water or soil when more trucks are employed to pick up recyclable products, air pollution will also increase.

(ii) Require Stricter and More Stringement Implementation

Recycling can have an adverse effect on health and the environment when not done properly. Debris and toxic waste that is improperly handled can contaminate land, air and the environment.

This is why more implementation must be followed. When recycling companies abandon dump sites, waste left lying around can have environmental effect.

(iii) Good Products are not Guaranteed

Not all recycled items are of high quality or even safe to use. As previously mentioned, recycled products may contain toxic chemicals that were previously present with the original material.

Digital Footprint

On the Internet, a digital footprint is the word used to describe the traces or footprints that people leave online. This is information transmitted online, such as forum registration, E-mails and attachments, uploaded videos or images and any other form of transmission of information all of which leaves traces of personal information about yourself available to others online. Digital footprints are created when personal data is released by the user for the purpose of sharing information about oneself on websites or social media.

There are two main classification of digital footprints:

(i) **Active digital footprint** When you intentionally put something online.

e.g.

- Posting on Facebook, Instagram, Snapchat, Twitter and other social media platforms.
- Filling out online forms, such as when signing up to receive E-mails or text.

(ii) **Passive digital footprint** When you have things about you online that you did not put on the Internet.

e.g.

- Websites that install cookies in your device without disclosing it to you.
- Apps and websites that use geolocation to pinpoint your location.

Digital Society and Netizen

In the era of digital society, our daily activities like communication, social networking, banking, shopping entertainment, education, transportation etc., are increasingly being driven by online transactions. Digital society thus reflects the growing trend of using digital technologies in all spheres of human activities. But while online, all of us need to be aware of how to conduct ourselves, how best to relate with others and what ethics, morals and values to maintain.

Anyone who uses digital technology along with Internet is a digital citizen or a netizen. A responsible netizen must abide by netiquettes, communication etiquettes and social media etiquettes.

Netiquette

The word netiquette is a combination of net (from Internet) and etiquette. It means respecting other user's views and displaying common etiquette when posting your views to online discussion groups. The need of netiquette arises mostly when sending or distributing e-mail posting on usenet groups or chatting.

Netiquette is short for "Internet etiquette". Etiquette is a code of polite behaviour in society while netiquette is a code of good behaviour on the Internet. This includes several aspects of the Internet, such as e-mail, social media, online chat, web forums, website comments and other types of online communication.

Below are the rules to follow for good netiquette:

(i) Avoid posting inframmatory or offensive comments online.

(ii) Respect other's privacy by not sharing personal information, photos or videos that another person may not want published online.

(iii) Never spam others by sending large amounts of unsolicited e-mail.

(iv) Do not troll people in web forums or website comments by repeatedly nagging or annoying them.

(v) Do not use offensive language.

(vi) Do not trust other when you are new.

(vii) Avoid replying to negative comments with more negative comments.

(viii) Stick to the topic when posting in online forums or when commenting on photos or videos such as YouTube or Facebook comments.

Communication Etiquettes

Digital communication includes Email, texting, instant messaging, talking on the cell phone, audio or video conferencing, posting on forums, social networking sites etc. Good communication over Email, chat room and other such forums require a digital citizen to abide by the communication etiquettes.

Below are the rules to follow for good communication etiquettes:

(i) We should not waste precious time in responding to unnecessary Emails or comments unless they have some relevance for us.

(ii) For concerns related to data and bandwidth, very large attachments may be avoided.

(iii) Whether the communication is synchronous or asynchronous, we should be polite and non-aggressive in our communication.

(iv) We should avoid being abusive even if we do not agree with other's point of view.

(v) We should be cautious while making a comment, replying or writing an email or forum post as such acts decide our credibility over a period of time.

Social Media Etiquettes

In the current digital era, we are familiar with different kinds of social media and we may have an account on Facebook, Google +, Twitter, Instagram, Pinterest or YouTube channel.

These platforms encourage users to share their thoughts and experiences through posts or pictures.

In this way, users can interact with other online users of those social media apps or channels.

In social media, there are certain etiquettes we need to follows

(i) Users should be wary of such possibilities and must know how to safeguard themselves and their accounts.

(ii) We need to be careful while befriending unknown people as their intentions possibly could be malicious and unsafe.

(iii) With experience, we should be able to figure out whether a news, message or post is genuine or fake.

(iv) We can upload almost anything on social network. However, remember that once uploaded, it is always there in the remote server even if we delete the files.

Phishing and Fraud E-mails

Phishing is an unlawful activity where fake websites or E-mails that look original or authentic are presented to the user to fraudulently collect sensitive and personal details, particularly usernames, passwords, banking and credit card details.

The most common phishing method is through E-mail spoofing where a fake email address is used and the user presumes it to be from an authentic source.

So you might get an email from an address that looks similar to your bank or educational institution, asking for your information, but if you look carefully you will see their URL address is fake. They will often use logo's of the original, making them difficult to detect from the original. Phishing attempts through phone calls or text messages are also common these days.

Chapter Practice

Objective Questions

• Multiple Choice Questions

1. Rishika found a crumpled paper under her desk. She picked it up and opened it. It contained some text which was struck off thrice. But she could still figure out easily that the struck off text was the E-mail ID and password of Garvit, her classmate. What is ethically correct for Rishika to do? **[NCERT]**

(a) Inform Garvit so that he may change his password.
(b) Give the password of Garvit's E-mail ID to all other classmates.
(c) Use Garvit's password to access his account.

Ans. (a) Inform Garvit so that he may change his password. Other options are incorrect because they are unethical in nature.

2. Suhana is down with fever. So, she decided not to go to school tomorrow. Next day, in the evening she called up her classmate, Shaurya and enquired about the computer class. She also requested him to explain the concept. Shaurya said, "Mam taught us how to use tuples in Python". Further, he generously said, "Give me some time; I will E-mail you the material which will help you to understand tuples in Python".

Shaurya quickly downloaded a 2-minute clip from the Internet explaining the concept of tuples in Python. Using video editor, he added the text "Prepared by Shaurya" in the downloaded video clip. Then, he emailed the modified video clip to Suhana. This act of Shaurya is an example of **[NCERT]**

(a) fair use   (b) hacking
(c) copyright infringement   (d) cybercrime

Ans. (c) Copyright infringement is when we use other person's work without taking their permission to use or we have not paid for it, if it is being sold. Suppose we download an image from the Internet and use it in our project. But if the owner of the copyright of the image does not permit its free usage, then using such an image even after giving reference of the image in our project is a violation of copyright.

3. After practicals, Atharv left the computer laboratory but forgot to sign off from his E-mail account. Later, his classmate Revaan started using the same computer. He is now logged in as Atharv. He sends inflammatory E-mail messages to few of his classmates using Atharv's E-mail account. Revaan's activity is an example of which of the following cybercrime? **[NCERT]**

(a) Hacking   (b) Identity theft
(c) Cyber bullying   (d) Plagiarism

Ans. (b) Because Revaan's use Atharv's E-mail account without Atharv's permission and he sends inflammatory E-mail messages few of his classmates using Atharv's E-mail account which is not good manners of user.

4. Self-repeating and do not require a computer program to attach themselves

(a) virus   (b) worms
(c) spyware   (d) ransomware

Ans. (b) A computer worm is a type of malware that spreads copies of itself from computer to computer. A worm can replicate itself without any human interaction, and it does not need to attach itself to a software program in order to cause damage.

5. A type of computer crime used to attack, steal user data, including login name, password and credit card numbers.

(a) Phishing
(b) Pharming
(c) Man-in-the-middle attack
(d) Cookies

Ans. (a) Phishing is a type of computer crime used to attack, steal user data, including login name, password and credit card numbers. Phishing starts with a fraudulent email or other communication that is designed to temptation a victim.

6. An attempt to harm, damage or cause threat to a system or network is broadly termed as

(a) cybercrime   (b) cyber attack
(c) cyber law   (d) digital crime

Ans. (b) Cyber attack is an umbrella term used to classify different computer & network attacks or activities such as extortion, identity theft, E-mail hacking, digital spying, stealing hardware, mobile hacking and physical security breaching.

7. Adware are pre-chosen ……… developed to display ads.
(a) banner
(b) software
(c) malware
(d) shareware

Ans. (b) Adware is software that is displayed on system or web pages for showing pre-chosen ads.

8. ………… is the kind of firewall is connected between the device and the network connecting to Internet.
(a) Hardware firewall
(b) Software firewall
(c) Stateful inspection firewall
(d) Microsoft firewall

Ans. (a) Hardware firewalls are those firewalls that need to be connected as additional hardware between the device through which the Internet is coming to the system and the network used for connecting to the Internet.

9. Firewall examines each ……… that are entering or leaving the Internal network.
(a) E-mails user
(b) updates
(c) connections
(d) data packets

Ans. (d) Firewalls examine each data packets that are entering or leaving the internal network which ultimately prevents unauthorised access.

10. What is cyber security?
(a) Provides security against malware
(b) Provides security against cyber-terrorists
(c) Protects a system from cyber attacks
(d) All of the above

Ans. (d) Cyber security provides security to a system against cyber-attacks by using various technologies and processes.

11. They are hackers and their main motive is to gain financial profit by doing cyber crimes. Who are "they" referred to here?
(a) White hat hackers
(b) Black hat hackers
(c) Hactivists
(d) Gray hat hackers

Ans. (b) Black hat hackers, often known as "crackers," are a sort of cyber crime that gain illegal access to a user's account or system in order to steal confidential data or introduce malware into the system for personal gain or to harm the company.

12. What is legal form of hacking known as?
(a) Hactivism
(b) Cracking
(c) Non-ethical hacking
(d) Ethical hacking

Ans. (d) Ethical hacking is a type of hacking used by white hat hackers to conduct penetration testing and discover possible dangers in businesses and organisations.

13. A software that can be freely accessed and modified.
(a) Synchronous software
(b) Package software
(c) OSS
(d) Middleware

Ans. (c) Software refers to a collection of programs. OSS stands for Open Source Software. It can be freely accessed, edited and modified according to our needs.

14. Which of the following is not an open source software?
(a) LibreOffice
(b) Microsoft Office
(c) GNU image manipulation
(d) MySQL

Ans. (b) MS-Office is not an open source software since its source code isn't shared publicly. Others like LibreOffice, MySQL are open source softwares through which is distributed along with its source code.

15. The user must agree to the ………… terms and agreements when they use an open source software.
(a) system
(b) license
(c) community
(d) programmer

Ans. (b) The user must agree to the license terms and agreement in order to access an open source software. There is a limitation of OSS that the users cannot modify the terms and conditions of any software.

16. Which of the following element make E-Waste hazardous in nature?
(a) Lead
(b) Glass
(c) Plastic
(d) Iron

Ans. (a) The presence of elements like lead, mercury, arsenic, cadmium, selenium, hexavalent chromium and flame retardants beyond threshold quantities make E-Waste hazardous in nature.

17. Which of these is not an example of cyber bullying?
(a) Copying a classmate's personal photo against his/her permission from his social media account and sending it to other friends on their E-mails.
(b) Bullying a classmate in the school corridor.
(c) Threatening someone on Whatsapp.
(d) Posting mean messages about someone on their social media.

Ans. (b) Cyber bullying is when someone uses technology to harass, threaten, embarrass or target another person. From given options, all are examples of cyber bullying except option (b). Bullying a classmate in a school corridor is not an example of cyber bullying.

18. Arun clicks on a link received in a message on his phone which promises him a complimentary trip to a destination of his choice. He forwarded this message to his friend, Panshul and asked him to do the same. But Panshul refuses and tells Arun that his personal and private information, such as online account names, login information and passwords can be stolen and he should be careful of such …………… attacks.
(a) phishing
(b) spamming
(c) scamming
(d) plagiarism

Ans. (a) He should be careful of such phishing attacks.
Phishing attacks are the practice of sending fraudulent communications that appear to come from a reputable source.

• Case Based MCQs

19. Geetika has recently created her social accounts. She is very excited as she waited so long to go online. She has recently also got admission in a prestigious high school and does not know many students.

When she logs into her social media a few days later, she finds that someone is posting negative, demeaning comments on her social media profile. She is also getting repeated mails from unknown people. Whenever she goes online, she is trolled by multiple unknown people.

Based on the given information, answer the following questions.

(i) Geetika is a victim of
   (a) eavesdropping
   (b) plagiarism
   (c) phishing
   (d) cyber stalking

(ii) Which of the following is the most appropriate action she should take?
   (a) She should stop going online and delete her social media accounts.
   (b) She should not share this with anyone as she might face more of such kind of behaviour.
   (c) She should file a complaint at the nearest police station.
   (d) She should inform her parents and bring to the notice of school authorities.

(iii) After hearing her ordeal, the school decides to publish a set of moral principles that determines the appropriate behaviour of students while using the Internet. The school is referring to................ .
   (a) intellectual property rights
   (b) internet privacy
   (c) computer ethics
   (d) cyber ethics

(iv) Geetika is advised by her best friend, Seerat to protect her personal information from intentional or unintentional attacks by others. This is also known as ....
   (a) digital right
   (b) copyright
   (c) data privacy
   (d) intellectual property

(v) The computer teacher of Geetika's class decides to take an online session on the topic Netiquettes, which generally includes
   (a) safeguarding one's passwords and sensitive online information
   (b) logging out of social media accounts after the session
   (c) not bullying or trolling anyone by disrespecting them or passing inappropriate remarks
   (d) All of the above

Ans. (i) (d) Geetika is a victim of cyber stalking. Cyber stalking refers to the use of Internet and other technologies to harass or stalk another person online. This is online harassment which is an extension of cyber bullying.

(ii) (d) She should inform her parents and bring to the notice of school authorities.

(iii) (d) The school is referring to cyber ethics. Cyber ethics refers to a code of safe and responsible behaviour for the Internet Community.

(iv) (c) This is also known as data privacy. Data privacy is a part of the data protection area that deals with the proper handling of data focusing on compliance with data protection regulations.

(v) (d) Netiquette means respecting other user's views and displaying common etiquette when posting your views to online discussion groups.

PART 2
Subjective Questions

• Short Answer Type Questions

1. What is cyber crime?

Ans. Cyber crime is a term for any illegal activity that uses a computer as its primary means of commission. Cyber crime encompasses any criminal act dealing with computers and networks. Additionally, cyber crime also includes traditional crimes conducted through the Internet. *For example,* Telemarketing and Internet fraud, identity theft and credit card account thefts are considered to be cybercrimes when the illegal activities are committed through the use of a computer and the Internet.

2. What do you mean by cyber stalking?

Ans. Cyber stalking is a crime in which the attacker harasses a victim using electronic communication, such as e-mail or Instant Messaging (IM), or messages posted to a website or a discussion group. Cyber stalking messages differ from ordinary spam in that a cyber stalker targets a specific victim with often threatening messages.

3. How can a virus is harmful for the computer system?

Ans. Virus causes damage to the data and files of a computer system. It can affect or attack any part of the computer software such as boot block, operating system, system areas, files and various application programs.

4. Give three guidelines to prevent the virus attack.

Ans. Three guidelines to prevent the virus attack are as follows:
   (i) Avoid to open unexpected e-mail attachments and downloads from unreliable sources. Resist the urge to double click everything in your mailbox.
   (ii) In stable reliable antivirus, scanning software and download its updates regularly.
   (iii) Scan files downloaded from the Internet or other external sources.

5. If your computer attacked by a trojan horse, what damage it may cause?

Ans. If computer attacked by a trojan horse, it can
  (i) Steal passwords   (ii) Copy sensitive data
  (iii) Carry out any other harmful operations etc.

6. Write four symptoms of a malware attack.

Ans. Some primary indications of a malware attack are
  (i) A program disappears from the computer even though you did not intentionally remove the program.
  (ii) An antivirus program cannot be installed on the computer, or the antivirus program will not run.
  (iii) You see unusual error messages.
  (iv) You cannot print items correctly.

7. Explain the digital form of signature.

Ans. Digital signature is an electronic form of a signature that can be attached to an electronically transmitted message and used to authenticate the identity of a sender.

8. Define password and also give the name of its two modes.

Ans. A password is an unspaced sequence of characters used to determine that a computer user requesting access to a computer system is really that particular user.
There are two common modes of password as follows
  (i) Weak password
  (ii) Strong password

9. What are the major factors that about the reasons behind plagiarism?

Ans. Following are the major factors about the reasons behind plagiarism :
  (i) Being lazy
  (ii) Lack of enforcement
  (iii) Fear of failure
  (iv) Not having enough knowledge
  (v) Lack of management skills

10. Privacy is the protection of personal information given online. In E-commerce, it is related to a company's policies on the use of user data.
  (i) Why is the above given statement important?
  (ii) What is the need to safeguard the user privacy?

Ans. (i) It is important for the safeguard of user privacy online.
  (ii) Online world is an open world and thus the personal information of a user must not be available openly, as it may be misused. Thus, it is very important and highly needed to safeguard user privacy.

11. Posing as someone else online and using his/her personal/financial information for shopping online or posting something is a common type of cyber crime these days.
  (i) What are such types of cyber crimes collectively called?
  (ii) What measures can you take to stop these?

Ans. (i) Online fraud
  (ii) The measures to stop these frauds may include:
    ■ A monitoring official body that ensures that sanctity of E-commerce company and delivery of goods/services as promised.
    ■ Strong security mechanism by the E-commerce site and payment gateways to prevent stealing of crucial information.

12. What do you mean by cookies?

Ans. Cookies are small text files that are saved in your web browser when you visit a website. The file might contain your login information, your user preferences, the contents of your online shopping cart and other identities. Your browser saves the cookies and notes the domain of the website that they belong to. Cookies can be first party and third party cookies. By default, first party cookies are allowed in every web browser. These are the cookies that store your own login id, password for some websites that you frequently visit.

Third party cookies are files stored on your computer from advertisers and other parties that have information sharing agreements with the site you visited.

13. Explain the guidelines about cyber ethics.

Ans. Following are few points which user should follow
  (i) **Honesty** As a part of decent behaviour (netiquette) user shall always demonstrate the truth while using Internet.
  (ii) **Respect** User should respect the privacy of the other users.
  (iii) **Confidentiality** User should keep confidentiality while using Internet and not share any information to anybody which will be breach and user should not try to get confidential data of other users.
  (iv) **Professionalism** User should maintain professional conduct and well mannered approach.
  (v) **Communication** User should ensure decent and polite communication with others.

14. What do you understand by confidentiality of information?

Ans. Confidentiality allows authorized users to access sensitive and protected data. It ensures that sensitive information are accessed only by an authorized person and kept away from those not authorized to possess them. It is implemented using security mechanisms such as usernames, passwords, access control lists (ACLs), and encryption.

15. Explain firewall.

Ans. A firewall is a network security device that monitors incoming and outgoing network traffic and decides whether to allow or block specific traffic based on a defined set of security rules.

The primary purpose of a firewall is to allow non-threatening traffic and prevent malicious or unwanted data traffic for protecting the computer from viruses and attacks.

A firewall is a cyber security tool that filters network traffic and helps users block malicious software from accessing the Internet in infected computers.

16. What do you mean by identity theft?

Ans. Identity thieves increasingly use personal information stolen from computers or computer networks, to commit fraud by using the data gained unlawfully. A user's identifiable personal data like demographic details, email ID, banking credentials, passport, PAN, Aadhaar number and various such personal data are stolen and misused by the hacker on behalf of the victim. This is one type of phishing attack where the intention is largely for monetary gain.

17. Explain software piracy.

Ans. Software piracy is the unauthorised use or distribution of software. Those who purchase a license for a copy of the software do not have the rights to make additional copies without the permission of the copyright owner. It amounts to copyright infringement regardless of whether it is done for sale, for free distribution or for copier's own use. One should avoid software piracy. Using pirated software not only degrades the performance of a computer system, but also affects the software industry which in turn affects the economy of a country.

18. Distinguish between active digital footprint and passive digital footprint.   **[NCERT]**

Ans. Differences between active digital footprint and passive digital footprint are as follows

Active digital footprint	Passive digital footprint
An active digital footprint is where the user has deliberately shared information about themselves either by using social media sites or by using websites.	A "passive digital footprint" is a data trail you unintentionally leave online.
The most obvious example is sharing information on social media, but email also contributes to your active footprint.	*For example*, your IP address, approximate location, or browser history.

19. What are differences between copyright and patent?   **[NCERT]**

Ans. Differences between copyright and patent are as follows

Copyright	Patent
Copyright has a longer validity of a lifetime of the owner and another sixty years after that.	A patent has a validity of 20 years, after which the invention is open to the public.
A copyright protects the expression of an idea	A patent protects the idea itself.
Copyright is another work of an already described design.	Patent works more on a design.

• Long Answer Type Questions

20. Write the various ways from which to avoid being stalked on social media.

Ans. There are various ways from being stalked on social media

  (i) **Hide your contacts** You should hide your contacts because a stalker may try to reach out to a friend of yours in order to get close to you.

  (ii) **Use security features** Keep your computer free from threats or breaches in security by installing safety software and a firewall.

  (iii) **Disable geotagging** It can be dangerous because a stalker can known where you are. So geotagging should be disable.

  (iv) **Make your profile private** Always make your profile private, to protect yourself from a stalker, set your setting to only share information.

  (v) **Delete an old account** You should delete your old account that are inactive.

21. What are the possible damages caused by viruses?

Ans. Computer viruses can cause and do the following damages

  (i) Delete or change files, documents, or even format your hard disk drive, making your computer unusable.

  (ii) A directory may be displayed as garbage.

  (iii) Display pictures.

  (iv) Slow down your PC dramatically.

  (v) Logical partitions created, partitions decrease in size.

  (vi) Release confidential information.

  (vii) Cause system to hang or freeze.

  (viii) Make strange noise or beeps.

  (ix) Create more than one partition.

22. Which guidelines are followed when choosing a password or setting up password?

Ans. Good criteria when choosing a password or setting up password, guidelines include the following

  (i) Do pick a word that you can easily remember.

  (ii) Do not pick a password that is similar to your previous password.

  (iii) Password should be mixture of letters digit.

  (iv) Always pick a word that can not be found in the dictionary.

  (v) It should not be easily guessed, example, not your birthday or maiden name etc.

23. Explain the rules for good netiquette.

Ans. Below are the rules to follow for good netiquette :

  (i) Avoid posting offensive comments online.

  (ii) Never spam others by sending large amounts of unsolicited E-mail.

  (iii) Don't troll people in web forums or website comments by repeatedly annoying them.

  (iv) Don't use offensive language.

  (v) Do not trust other when you are new.

  (vi) Avoid replying to negative comments with more negative comments.

  (vii) Stick the topic when posting in online forums or when commenting on photos or videos such as YouTube or Facebook comments.

24. What do you mean by virus and malware? Explain any two types of malware in detail.

Ans. Malware is a general term used for all the unwanted softwares which usually disturbs the balance or the behaviour of the computer. Under which all the malicious software comes such as virus, worms, spyware, adware etc.

Whereas, virus is one of the malicious software or you could say one of the type of malware which can cause damage to the data and files which are saved in the respective system. The main or the dangerous thing about virus is that it can affect or attack any part of the computer software such as the boot block, operating system, system areas, files and applications.

Viruses can do the following things in a system
 (i) Damage data files
 (ii) Destroy files
 (iii) Make disc unreadable
 (iv) Cause damage they weren't designed to.

Some of the malware are described below

Worms A worm is a common malware which mainly corrupts the network access to the computer. It is a standalone malware computer program that replicates itself to other computers through the network. Unlike a computer virus, it does not need to attach itself to an existing program.

Trojan A trojan horse, is a non-self-replicating type of malware which represents itself as a harmless, useful gifts, in order to persuade victims to install them on their computers and after getting installed they do not perform the task they were representing, instead they start corrupting the system functionality.

25. What are the specific usage rules that can help you to protect yourself on social networking sites?

Ans. There are various tips, with the help of these you can protect yourself on social networking sites as:
 (i) **Be cautious about how much personal information you provide on social networking sites** A common way for cyber criminals to break into your account is by clicking the 'Forget password' link. The answer to your security question could be found in your profile or it could be found in one of your posts. The more information you provide, the easier it is for hacker to steal your identity.
 (ii) **Precautions taken when you click on links** Even if these links are in a message from your friend, be cautious when clicking on the link. It could be the case where your friend's account has been hacked. It is sending malicious links to everyone on their contact list.
 (iii) **Be selective on who you accept as a friend on your social network** Identity thieves might create fake profiles in order to get information from you. People are not always who say they are.
 (iv) **Type the address of your social networking sites directly into your browser** If you click a link that leads you to a social networking website through an e-mail or another website, it may actually be a phishing website. It is design to look like the legal website in order to

trick users into providing their user name and password. This does not apply only to social networking sites but any links you receive *via* e-mail or any other website.
 (v) **Whatever you post online is permanent** Whatever information you posted on your social networking site is permanent. So, think twice before you post anything on social networking site.
 (vi) **Customise privacy settings** Use privacy settings to control who can see various aspects of your personal information.
 (vii) **Never use the same password for all your account** This applies not only to social networking sites but to all your online accounts. This ensures that a violation in one of your accounts does not put your other accounts at risk.
 (viii) **Be careful when you install third party applications on your social networking sites** Many social networking sites allow you to download third party applications that let you do more with your personal page. However, cyber criminals can make use of these applications to steal your personal information without your knowledge.

26. Criminal activities or offences carried out in a digital environment can be considered as cybercrime. In such crimes, either the computer itself is the target or the computer is used as a tool to commit a crime. Cybercrimes are carried out against either an individual, or a group, or an organisation or even against a country, with the intent to directly or indirectly cause physical harm, financial loss or mental harassment.

Based on the above information, answer the following questions.
 (i) What is/are the object(s) of crime?
 (ii) Given an example of cyber crime.
 (iii) What do you mean by hacker?
 (iv) Name two most common cyber crimes.
 (v) Where is most series computer crimes commited?

Ans. (i) Hacking, phishing and spamming
 (ii) Illegally transferring large sums of money to their own accounts.
 (iii) Criminals who perform computer related illegal activities are often referred to as hackers.
 (iv) (a) Cyber bullying (b) Cyber trolling
 (v) In banking and financial service industries.

Chapter Test

Multiple Choice Questions

1. Charlene is an artist. She displays her artwork on the Internet using her website to attract buyers. One day while browsing the Internet she discovers that another artist has displayed her painting portraying it as his own. Which rights of Charlene was infringed?

(a) Digital Privacy Rights
(b) Intellectual Property Rights
(c) Digital Property Rights
(d) Intellectual Privacy Rights

2. Shreya told her friend Princy about a term that, "It is the study of ethics pertaining to computers, encompassing user behaviour and what computers are programmed to and how this affects individuals and society". What is it?

(a) Cyber ethics
(b) Plagiarism
(c) Netiquette
(d) Hacking

3. Which of the following refers to attempt to gain information from undisclosed areas?

(a) Hacking
(b) Knowledge
(c) Etiquette
(d) Plagiarism

4. Rahul is working in MNC company. His friend told him about a term that it encourages people to create new softwares as well as helps them to improve the existing application. Identify that term.

(a) Hacking
(b) Plagiarism
(c) Intellectual property rights
(d) Netiquette

5. .... footprints which include data that we intentionally submit online.

(a) Active digital
(b) Passive digital
(c) Both (a) and (b)
(d) None of these

Short Answer Type Questions

6. What do you mean by digital footprint?

7. How can you explain netizen?

8. What is intellectual property and how can protect these rights?

9. Define two popular categories of public licenses.

10. What is non-ethical hacker? Also, give its other name.

Long Answer Type Questions

11. What is identity theft? Also, give its few examples.

12. Explain the preventing cyber crime.

13. Define the reduce and recycle factors used in E-Waste management.

Answers

Multiple Choice Questions

1. (b) 2. (a) 3. (a) 4. (c) 5. (a)

For Detailed Solutions
Scan the code

Practice Paper 1*
(Solved)

1. Suppose that the list
```
list1 = [2,3,4,7,53,23,12,9,0]
```
Based on the above information, answer the following questions.

(i) Identify the output of following code.
```
l = list1. pop(9)
print(l)
```
  (a) [2, 3, 4, 7, 53, 23, 12, 0]   (b) [2, 3, 4, 7, 53, 23, 12, 9]
  (c) 9   (d) Error

(ii) Choose the correct output from the following options for statement list1[−4].
  (a) 7   (b) 53
  (c) 23   (d) 63

(iii) Identify the output of following code.
```
print (list1[5 :])
```
  (a) [23, 12, 9, 0]   (b) [53, 23, 12, 9, 0]
  (c) [2, 3, 4, 7, 53]   (d) [2, 3, 4, 7, 53, 23]

(iv) Which command will be used to add a new element 14 to a list list1?
  (a) `list1.append(14)`   (b) `list1.add(14)`
  (c) `list1.addLast(14)`   (d) `list1.addEnd(14)`

(v) Which value is used to represent the second index of list 1?
  (a) 2   (b) 1
  (c) −2   (d) −1

2. Find the output of the given questions.

```
L1 = [1, 2, 3, 4]
L2 = [5, 6, 7, 8]
```
  (i) `print (L2[2])`

  (ii) `print (L1+L2)`

  (iii) `print (len (L1*2))`

  (iv) `print (L1[4])`

  (v) `print (L2[-3])`

  (vi) `print (L2[:3])`

3. Define the concatenate lists with an example.

Or Find the output of the given questions.

```
tup1 = (23,45,23,12,(12,14,16),34)
```
  (i) `print (tup1[4])`

  (ii) `tup1[1 : 8 : 2]`

  (iii) `tup1[2] + tup 1[-3]`

4. Write a code to add all the items in a dictionary.

```
dic1 = {'One'  : 20,'Two' : 15, 'Three' : 10, 'Four' : 12 }
```
Or Define the get() method used in dictionary.

5. Give any three guidelines to avoid plagiarism.

6. Define the following terms :

  (i) Softlifting

  (ii) Renting

  (iii) Hard disk loading

Or What is passive digital footprint? Also, give its two examples.

7. Write a program to calculate the average of the elements which are entered by user.

Or Write a Python program to count the even and odd numbers in a tuple.

8. What points should be considered as safety measures to reduce the risk of cyber crime ?

Or How to avoid being stalked on social media by disable geotagging, delete old accounts and hide your contacts?

9. Explain cyber stalking with its any three examples.

Or Explain online fraud. How to ensure safe sites, while entering crucial information?

EXPLANATIONS

1. (i) (*d*) In pop(9), parentheses put index number instead of element. In the given list, maximum index number is 8, then 9 is out of index range.

  (ii) (*c*) −1 corresponds to the last index in the list , −2 represents the second last element and so on.

    So, the correct output for statement list1 [−4] is 23.

  (iii) (*a*) To print elements from specific index till the end, use [Index:], so list1 [5:] will print from index number 5 till end.

  (iv) (*a*) append () method is used to add a new element to a list. So, correct command is

```
list1. append (14)
```

  (v) (*b*) To access the list's elements, index number is used. The index number should be an integer. Index of 0 refers to first element, 1 refers to second element and so on.

2. (i) 7

  (ii) [1, 2, 3, 4, 5, 6, 7, 8]

  (iii) 8

  (iv) IndexError

  (v) 6

  (vi) [5, 6, 7]

3. In Python, to perform on the list concatenation, the use of '+' operator can easily add the whole of one list to other list.

e.g.

```
l1 = [1, 2, 3]
l2 = [3, 4, 5]
l = l1 + l2
print(l)
```

Output

[1, 2, 3, 3, 4, 5]

Or

  (i) (12, 14, 16)

  (ii) (45, 12, 34)

  (iii) 35

4.
```
dic1 =
{'One':20,'Two':15,'Three':10,'Four':12}
sum = 0
for key in dic1:
    sum = sum + dic1 [key]
print (sum)
```

Or

get () method returns the value for the given key, if present in the dictionary. It takes maximum of two parameters.

Syntax `dictionary_name. get (key [, value])`

Here, key to be searched in the dictionary value (optional) to be returned, if the key not found. The default value is None.

5. Follow the below given guidelines to avoid plagiarism:

  (i) To avoid plagiarism, instead of copying the language of the book as it is, try to put it in your own language/words.

  (ii) One should have a clear understanding of plagiarism and its consequences, so that no one can perform it unintentionally.

  (iii) If copying someone else's work in our task, word for word, then do not forget enclosing it in quotes and also mention its source.

6. (i) **Softlifting** Purchasing only one licensed copy of a software and distributing and loading it onto multiple systems is called softlifting.

  (ii) **Renting** Selling of a software illegally for temporary use as on rent basis is called renting.

  (iii) **Hard Disk Loading** Installing an illegal copy of software on the hard disk of a personal computer is called hard disk loading.

Or

Passive digital footprint done when you have things about you online that you did not put on the Internet.

e.g.

  (i) Websites that install cookies in your device without disclosing it to you.

  (ii) Apps and websites that use geolocation to pinpoint your location.

7.
```
list1 = list()
add = 0
num = int (input ("Enter the number of
elements:"))
print ("Enter the number:")
for i in range (int (num)):
    l = int (input (""))
    list1. append (int (l))
    add = add + list1[i]
average =  add /num
print ("Average =", average)
```

Or

```
tuple1 = (23,45,88,24,21,44,33,51)
even = 0
odd = 0
for i in tuple 1 :
    if i %2 == 0 :
        even = even +1
    else:
        odd = odd +1
print ("Even number in the tuple :" , even)
print ("Odd number in the tuple :", odd)
```

8. Do not visit or download anything from untrusted websites.

- Always secure wireless network at home with strong password and regularly change it.

- Use an antivirus software and keep it updated always.

- Use strong password for web logic and change it periodically. Ignore common words or names in password.

- Always update the system software which include the Internet browser and other application software.

- Take a regular backup of important data.

Or

- **Disable Geotagging** Geotagging automatically shows your location from your smartphone. This can be dangerous because a stalker can know where you are. So, you should turn OFF all location and geotagging services for social media.

- **Delete Old Accounts** If you have old accounts that are currently inactive, delete them. This is especially important if the sites have personal information or photos of you.

- **Hide Your Contacts** If you have a friend list on your social media account, hide it. A stalker may try to reach out to a friend of yours in order to get close to you.

9. Cyber stalking is a form of cyber crime that takes place online when a criminal uses technology to harass or threaten a person or an organisation. Cyber stalking is often including by real time or offline stalking. A stalker may be an online stranger or a person whom the target knows. Examples of cyber stalking are

   - Hacking and saving E-mails, text messages and social media posts and using them to harass or blackmail a victim.

   - Hacking into the victim's social media account to post offensive material and comments.

   - Creating malicious websites, fake social media profiles and blogs about a victim.

Or

Fraud using the Internet is online fraud or Internet fraud. It is a type of fraud or deception which makes use of the Internet and could involve hiding of information or providing incorrect information for the purpose of tricking victims out of money, property and inheritance.

Before entering private information such as passwords or credit card details on a website you can ensure that the link is secure in three ways

(i) There should be a padlock symbol in the browser window, that appears when you attempt to log in or register.

(ii) The web address should begin with 'https : //' where 's' stands for secure.

(iii) Type the URL of the website in the address bar of the browser on your own. Do not click on a link that takes to this website or do not cut/copy the link of this website and paste it.

Practice Paper 2*
(Solved)

General Instructions

- **Time :** 2 Hours
- **Max. Marks :** 35

1. There are 9 questions in the question paper. All questions are compulsory.
2. Question no. 1 is a Case Based Question, which has five MCQs. Each question carries one mark.
3. Question no. 2-6 are Short Answer Type Questions. Each question carries 3 marks.
4. Question no. 7-9 are Long Answer Type Questions. Each question carries 5 marks.
5. There is no overall choice. However, internal choices have been provided in some questions. Students have to attempt only one of the alternatives in such questions.

As exact Blue-print and Pattern for CBSE Term II exams is not released yet. So the pattern of this paper is designed by the author on the basis of trend of past CBSE Papers. Students are advised not to consider the pattern of this paper as official, it is just for practice purpose.

1. Suppose that the tuple

```
tup1=(1,2,3,(4,5),6,(7,8,9),10)
```

Based on the above information, answer the following questions.

(i) Identify the correct output of the following code.

```
print (tup1 [2 : 4])
```

  (a) (3, (4, 5))   (b) (2, 3)   (c) (3, (4, 5), 6)   (d) Error

(ii) Find the value of tup1 [2. 5].

  (a) 3   (b) (4, 5)   (c) (7, 8, 9)   (d) Error

(iii) Choose the correct output for tup1 [9].

  (a) 9   (b) 10

  (c) (7, 8, 9)   (d) Error

(iv) Choose the correct output for len (tup1).

  (a) 10   (b) 7

  (c) 8   (d) Error

(v) Identify the output of tup1 [5:].

  (a) ((7, 8, 9), 10)   (b) (7, 8, 9, 10)

  (c) (6, (7, 8, 9), 10)   (d) Error

2. What will be the output of the following code?

```
list1 = [12, 10, 15, 13, 14, 22, 37]
for i in range (0, len (list1)):
    if i% 2 ! = 0 :
        print (list 1 [i])
```

3. What will be the output of the following code ?

```
num = { }
num [(1, 2, 4)] = 18
num [(4, 2, 1)] = 16
num [ (1, 3)] = 24
sum = 0
for k in num :
    sum + = num [k]
print (len (num) + sum)
```

Or Define the following terms with respect to tuples.

    (i) sorted ()   (ii) reversed ()

  (iii) any ()

4. Answer the following questions.

    (i) t1 = (1, 2, 3, (4, (5, 6)), 7, (8, 9))

       len(t1)

   (ii) t1 = (4,)

       t2 = ()

       t = t1 + t2

       any(t)

  (iii) t1 = (1, 2, 3, (4, (3, 6)), 3, (8, 3)) t1.count(3)

Or What do you mean by nested dictionary?

5. Write any three features to protect of intellectual property rights of individuals.

6. How can spyware harm you?

Or What is open source software? What criteria must be met to be considered as open source software?

7. Write a program to read a list of n integers. Create two new lists, one having all even numbers and the other having all odd numbers from the given list.

Or Find output of the given Python program to swap keys and values in dictionary.

```
dict1 = {'First': 50,'Second': 145,'Third': 150,'Fourth':170,'Fifth':160,'Sixth': 75}
d1 = dict ([(value, key) for key, value in dict1. items()])
print ("Original dictionary is:")
print (dict1)
print ()
print ("Dictionary after swapping is:")
print ("keys : value")
for i in d1:
    print (i,":", d1 [i])
```

8. Define the form of software piracy.

Or What is digital communication? What are the rules to follow for good communication etiquettes?

9. What is scam? Also, write important things to keep in mind while using the Internet to avoid scam?

Or Explain IT Act 2000 with its objectives.

EXPLANATIONS

1. (i) (*a*) (:) is a slice operator, which returns the sub-part of any data type as string, list, tuple etc.

Index number is started from 0, so the value of index number 2 is '3' and this will display the element till last index number −1 i.e. $(4 - 1 =) 3$.

So, the correct output is (3, (4, 5)).

(ii) (*d*) It will give TypeError because tuple's index must be integers or slices, not float.

(iii) (*d*) It will give IndexError because tuple index is out of range. Its maximum index is 6 because index is started from 0 but in tup1 [9] asked about index number 9, so it will give an error.

(iv) (*b*) len() is used to count the number of elements that present in the tuple. Given tuple is a nested tuple, so (4, 5) will considered as one element and (7, 8, 9) will considered as one element.

Then, this will give 7 as output.

(v) (*a*) To display elements from specific index till the end, use [index:], so tup1 [5:] will display the elements from index number 5 to till end i.e. ((7, 8, 9), 10).

2. Output

```
10
13
22
```

3. Output

```
61
```

Or (i) **sorted** () is used to sort the given tuple in ascending order. But this method returns the elements in square brackets.

(ii) **reversed** () allows us to process the items in a sequence in reverse order. It accepts a sequence and returns an iterator.

(iii) **any** () returns True if atleast one element is present in the tuple, otherwise returns False.

4. (i) 6   (ii) True   (iii) 2

Or Nested dictionary means putting a dictionary inside another dictionary. Nesting is of great use as kind of information we can model in programs expanded greatly.

Syntax

```
Nested_dict = {'dict A' : {key1 : value1},
'dictB' : {key2: value2}}
```

Here, Nested_dict is a nested dictionary with the dictionary dictA and dictB. They are two dictionaries and each having own key and value.

5. The protection of intellectual property right of individuals lead to following features

(i) It encourages people to create new software as well as helps them to improve the existing applications.

(ii) An environment is provided for the innovative thoughts and technologies.

(iii) Provides the assurity of good returns, people and businesses invest in the national economy.

6. Spyware can harm you in many ways such as

- Malware will log your keystrokes.
- Steal your passwords.
- Observe your browsing choices.
- Spawn pop-up windows.
- Send your targeted E-mail.
- Redirect your web browser to phishing pages.
- Report your personal information to distant servers.
- Can alter your computer settings (like web browser home page settings or the placement of your desktop icons).
- Can affect the performance of your computer system.

Or Open source software is any computer software that is distributed with its source code available for modification e.g. Linux, Unix, MySQL, etc.

To be considered as open source software, certain criteria must be met as follows:

Software must be available free or at a low cost.

Source code must be included.

Anyone must be allowed to modify the source code.

7.
```
list1 = []
even = []
odd = []
num = int (input ("Enter the number of
elements:"))
for i in range (1, num + 1):
    value = int (input("Enter the element
:"))
    list1. append (value)
for j in range (num) :
    if (list1 [j] % 2 == 0):
        even. append (list1 [j])
    else:
        odd. append (list1 [j])
print ("Element in Even list is :", even)
print ("Element in Odd list is :", odd)
```

Or **Output**

Original dictionary is :

{'First' : 50, 'Second':145, 'Third':150, 'Fourth':170, 'Fifth':160, 'Sixth':75}

Dictionary after swapping is :

keys	:	value
50	:	First
145	:	Second
150	:	Third
170	:	Fourth
160	:	Fifth
75	:	Sixth

8. The following are the forms of software piracy:

(i) **Software Counterfeiting** This type of software piracy occurs when fake copies of software are produced in such a way that they appear to be authentic.

(ii) **Softlifting** Purchasing only one licensed copy of a software and distributing and loading it onto multiple systems is called softlifting.

(iii) **Renting** Selling of a software illegally for temporary use as on rent basis is called renting.

(iv) **Hard Disk Loading** Installing an illegal copy of software on the hard disk of a personal computer is called hard disk loading.

(v) **Uploading and Downloading** Creating duplicate copies of the licensed software or uploading and downloading it from the Internet.

Or Digital communication includes E-mail, texting, instant messaging, talking on the cell phone, audio or video conferencing, posting on forums, social networking sites etc.

Below are the rules to follow for good communication etiquettes :

(i) For concerns related to data and bandwidth, very large attachments may be avoided.

(ii) We should avoid being abusive even if we do not agree with other's point of view.

(iii) We should not waste precious time in responding to unnecessary E-mails or comments unless they have some relevance for us.

(iv) Whether the communication is synchronous or asynchronous, we should be polite and non-aggressive in our communication.

9. A scam is a term used to describe any fraudulent business or scheme that takes money or other goods from an unsuspecting person.

Important things to keep in mind while using the Internet to avoid scam include the following :

(i) Do not click on any link in a mail that tells you to change any of your password or any security code.

(ii) If you want to make payments online and you are afraid of using your ATM/credit card details so that they will not be stolen. The first thing, you want to be aware of is that when you click on a page to make payments, that page must be secured and it must start with https:// where 's' after that http refers to secured and there must be a padlock sign at the bottom of that window by the right side.

(iii) Never reply to E-mail from any unknown or unreliable source.

(iv) Never respond to an E-mail or advertisement claiming you have won something.

Or Information technology is application of computers and telecommunication equipment store, retrieve, transmit and manipulate data. IT is generally not used in reference to personal or home computing and networking. IT refers to anything related to computing technology, such as networking, hardware, software, Internet or the people that work with these technologies.

Objectives of IT Act

- To stop computer crime and protect privacy of Internet users.
- To make more power to IPO, RBI and Indian evidence Act for restricting electronic crime.
- To give legal recognition for keeping books of accounts by bankers and other companies in electronic form.
- To give legal recognition to digital signature for accepting any agreement *via* computer.
- To provide facility of filling document online relating to school admission or registration in employment exchange.
- To give legal recognition to any transaction which is done by electronic way or use of Internet.

Practice Paper 3*
(Solved)

General Instructions

■ Time : 2 Hours
■ Max. Marks : 35

1. There are 9 questions in the question paper. All questions are compulsory.
2. Question no. 1 is a Case Based Question, which has five MCQs. Each question carries one mark.
3. Question no. 2-6 are Short Answer Type Questions. Each question carries 3 marks.
4. Question no. 7-9 are Long Answer Type Questions. Each question carries 5 marks.
5. There is no overall choice. However, internal choices have been provided in some questions. Students have to attempt only one of the alternatives in such questions.

As exact Blue-print and Pattern for CBSE Term II exams is not released yet. So the pattern of this paper is designed by the author on the basis of trend of past CBSE Papers. Students are advised not to consider the pattern of this paper as official, it is just for practice purpose.

1. Consider the following dictionary:

```
dic1 = {10:(45,12,8),'One':[32,44,56]}
```

Based on the above code, answer the following questions.

(i) Choose the correct option of given statement.

```
print(dic1.values())
```

(a) dict_values ([(45, 12, 8), [32, 44, 56]])　(b) ([45, 12, 8], [32, 44, 56])
(c) values ([32, 44, 56], (45, 12, 8))　(d) dict ([32, 44, 56], (45, 12, 8))

(ii) Each key is separated by which symbol?

(a) ;　(b) :　(c) ,　(d) @

(iii) Which output is best suited for given statement?

```
dic1.get('One')
```

(a) (32, 44, 56)　(b) [32, 44, 56]　(c) 32, 44, 56　(d) Error

(iv) Identify the output of len (dic1).

(a) 2　(b) 8　(c) 4　(d) 6

(v) Find the output of following code.

```
>>> dic1. clear()
>>> dic1
```

(a) {}　(b) Empty dictionary message
(c) None　(d) Error

2. What will be the output of the following code segment?

```
list 1 = [10, 20, 30, 40, 50, 60, 70, 80, 90, 100]
```

(i) `del list1 [3:]`

```
   print(list1)
```

(ii) `del list1 [:5]`
   `print(list1)`

(iii) `del list1 [::2]`
   `print (list1)`

Or Observe the following tuple and answer the questions that follow.

`tuple1 = (10, 20,'One', 'Two', 30, (40, 50),'Three')`

(i) `len (tuple1)`

(ii) `tuple1 [-6]`

(iii) `tuple1 [3]`

(iv) `tuple1 [: 2]`

(v) `tuple [3 :]`

(vi) `tuple1 [1 : 8 : 2]`

3. Predict the output.

```
dic1 = {}
dic1 [1] = 2
dic1 ['1'] = 4
dic1 [1.0] = 8
sum = 0
for i in dic1:
    sum = sum+ dic1 [i]
print (sum)
print (dic1)
```

Or Define the insert () method of list with an example.

4. What is dictionary? Also, write the ways to delete elements from a dictionary.

5. Define the ways to stop online frauds.

Or Explain the identity protection while using Internet.

6. What is active digital footprint? Write any two examples of it.

7. Write Python program to count the frequencies in a list using dictionary.

Or Write the best suited method's name for the following conditions.

(i) Calculate the sum of all the elements.

(ii) Calculate the total occurrence of given element of list.

(iii) Returns the index of first occurrence.

(iv) Calculate the total length of list.

(v) Used to remove all the items of a list.

8. What are Intellectual Property Rights (IPR)? Also, explain Patent is one of the types of IPR.

Or Explain E-Waste disposal management.

9. What is digital footprint? Also, write the differences between active digital footprint and passive digital footprint.

Or Define the following terms :

(i) Hacking   (ii) Piracy

(iii) Cyber crime   (iv) Plagiarism

(v) Netiquette

EXPLANATIONS

1. (i) (*a*) values () returns a view object that displays a list of all the values in the dictionary. It does not take any parameters.

(ii) (*c*) Each key value pair in a dictionary is separated by a colon (:) whereas each key is separated by a comma (,). In which, key will be a single element and values can be list or list within a list, numbers etc.

(iii) (*b*) get () method returns the value for the given key, if present in the dictionary. It takes maximum of two parameters.

(iv) (*a*) len () method is used to return the total length of the dictionary. It counts the number of keys present in the dictionary.

(v) (*a*) clear () is used to remove the elements of the dictionary. It produces an empty dictionary.

2. (i) [10, 20, 30]

(ii) [60, 70, 80, 90, 100]

(iii) [20, 40, 60, 80, 100]

Or (i) 7

(ii) 20

(iii) 'Two'

(iv) (10, 20)

(v) ('Two', 30, (40, 50), 'Three')

(vi) (20, 'Two', (40, 50))

3. l2

{'1 : 4', '1.0' : 8}

Or insert () method is used to insert an element at specified position in the list. This method takes two arguments : one for index number and second for element value.

Syntax

```
list_name. insert (index, element)
e.g. l1 = [1,2,3,4]
l1. insert (2, 10)
print (l1)
```

Output

[1, 2, 10, 3, 4]

4. Dictionary is an unordered collection of data values that stored the key: value pair instead of single value as an element.

There are following ways to delete elements from a dictionary as follows :

(i) **Using del keyword** This keyword is used to delete the key that is present in the dictionary.

Syntax `del dictionary_name [key]`

(ii) **Using pop () method** This method is used to delete key and respective value from dictionary.

Syntax `dictionary_name.pop (key)`

5. (i) Strong security mechanism by the E-commerce site and payment gateways to prevent stealing of crucial information.

(ii) A monitoring official site that ensures the sancity of E-commerce company and delivery of goods services as promised.

(iii) Official guidelines and safeguards on selling of user's data to third parties.

Or Your personal identity is important as it defines who you are. Your identity includes your personal information such as name, address, contact information, bank account, credit card numbers and social security numbers should be kept private. We surf the internet for a variety of reasons from using social media, buying and selling goods etc., and many more. When we give out our private data to businesses and other internet users such as while filling forms or making payment etc., we trust them to use that information for appropriate purposes.

This is not always the case though and financial and personal data can be used for harmful reasons such as hacking, stalking and identity fraud. Identity fraud is when personal details that have accessed or stolen are used to commit fraudulent acts.

6. Active digital footprint done when you intentionally put something online.

e.g.

(i) Posting on Facebook, Instagram, Snapchat, Twitter and other social media platforms.

(ii) Filling out online forms, such as when signing up to receive E-mails or text.

7.
```
lst = []
n = int (input("Enter number of elements:"))
for i in range (0, n):
    ele = int (input ())
    lst . append (ele)
print ("Original list :", lst)
print ("Elements with their frequency")
freq = {}
for item in lst :
    if (item in freq):
        freq [item] + = 1
else :
freq [item]=1
for key, value in freq. items ():
    print ("% d : % d"% (key, value))
```

Or (i) sum ()

(ii) count ()

(iii) index ()

(iv) len ()

(v) clear ()

8. Intellectual Property Rights (IPR) are the rights given to persons over the creations of their minds. Common types of IPR include copyright, trademarks, patents, industries design rights and in some jurisdictions trade secrets.

Patent It is usually granted for inventions. Unlike copyright, the inventor needs to apply (file) for patenting the invention. When a patent is granted, the owner gets an exclusive right to prevent others from using, selling or distributing the protected invention. Patent gives full control to the patentee to decide whether or how the invention can be used by others. Thus, it encourages inventors to share their scientific or technological findings with other. A patent protects an invention for 20 years, after which it can be freely used.

Or Some of the feasible methods of E-Waste management are reduce, reuse and recycle.

   (i) **Reduce** We should try to reduce the generation of E-Waste by purchasing the electronic or electrical devices only according to our need. Also, they should be used to their maximum capacity and discarded only after their useful life has ended. Good maintenance of electronics devices also increases the life of the devices.

  (ii) **Reuse** It is the process of reusing the electronic or electric waste after slight modification. The electronic equipment that is still functioning should be donated or sold to someone who is still willing to use it. The process of reselling old electronic goods at lower prices is called refurbishing.

 (iii) **Recycle** Recycling is the process of conversion of electronic devices into something that can be used again and again in some or the other manner. Only those products should be recycled that cannot be repaired, refurbished or reused. To promote recycling of E-Waste many companies and NGOs are providing door-to-door pick up facilities for collecting the E-Waste from homes and offices.

9. On the Internet, a digital footprint is the word used to describe the traces or footprints that people leave online. This is information transmitted online, such as forum registration, E-mails and attachments, uploaded videos or images and any other form of transmission of information all of which leaves traces of personal information about yourself available to others online. Digital footprints are created when personal data is released by the user for the purpose of sharing information about oneself on websites or social media.

Active digital footprint	Passive digital footprint
Active digital footprint is where the user has deliberately shared information about themselves either by using social media sites or by using websites.	Passive digital footprint is a data trail you unintentionally leave online.
It would be where a user has been online and information has been stored on an online database.	When you visit a website, the web server may log your IP address, which identifies your Internet service provider and your approximate location.

Or (i) Hacking refers to the misuse of devices like computers, smartphones, tablets and networks to cause damage to or corrupt systems, gather information on users, steal data and documents or disrupt data-related activity.

  (ii) Piracy refers to the unauthorised duplication of copyrighted content that is then sold at substantially lower prices in the 'grey' market. The ease of access to technology has meant that over the years, piracy has become more rampant.

 (iii) Cyber crime is also called computer crime. The use of a computer as an instrument to further illegal ends, such as committing fraud, trafficking in child pornography and intellectual property, stealing identities or violating privacy.

 (iv) Plagiarism is presenting someone else's work or ideas as your own, with or without their consent, by incorporating it into your work without full acknowledgement.

  (v) Netiquette is short for "Internet etiquette". Just like etiquette is a code of polite behavior in society, netiquette is a code of good behavior on the Internet. This includes several aspects of the Internet, such as E-mail, social media, online chat, web forums, website comments, multiplayer gaming and other types of online communication .

Printed by Libri Plureos GmbH in Hamburg,
Germany